ENDORSEMENTS

As a popular speaker and longtime radio host, Ron's voice and practical wisdom are known to many. But this is my friend Ron as you've never heard him—with a depth of compassion, honesty, and hope that can only come from a heart that has been broken...and then flooded with hope.

—**Josh D. McDowell**, author

As has been his trademark for decades, Ron attacks the gritty reality of grief in a way that not only reveals his heart but also offers biblical insight and peace to anyone suffering heartache from any source. Ron unflinchingly casts himself into the embrace of the God of all comfort.

—**Jerry B. Jenkins**, novelist and biographer,
coauthor of the Left Behind series

This is a great book, readable, honest, and biblical. A healing balm for those who are suddenly thrust into a bleak future and left only with memories of happier times. Thanks, Ron, for this window into your life that gives us a ray of hope in our sorrow and the reminder that, despite our losses, we still have God and His promises. Read this book for yourself and pass it along to a friend.

—**Dr. Erwin W. Lutzer**, pastor emeritus,
The Moody Church, Chicago

As followers of Jesus, we have the blessing of knowing that this broken world isn't all there is. Through touching personal stories and his own poignant experiences of brokenness and loss, Ron repeatedly shares the source of our *defiant hope*: Jesus Christ. If you have experienced traumatic loss, I encourage you to read *Hope When Your Heart is Breaking* and cling to the biblical promises Ron offers.

—**Will Graham**, executive director of the Billy
Graham Training Center at The Cove

When Ron Hutchcraft writes a book, you can be sure it contains both biblical truth and spiritual inspiration. *Hope When Your Heart is Breaking* will lift all our hearts during the difficult seasons of our lives.

—**Jim Cymbala**, pastor, The Brooklyn Tabernacle

I know firsthand the pain of loss when plans change, relationships end, and loved ones die. In *Hope When Your Heart Is Breaking*, my friend Ron Hutchcraft reminds us through Scripture that God is still good. And God is still Hope. This is more than a book—it's a lifeline.

—**Nick Hall**, founder and chief communicator, *Pulse*

We all have a need for hope. But where is hope when the unexpected happens? Our friend Ron writes about his heartbreak with unvarnished honesty—it's real, but so is his needed help, leading us hand in hand to the place of renewed hope. Yes, we all have a need for *this kind of hope!*

—**June Hunt**, founder and chief servant officer, Hope For The Heart and The Hope Center; author

All of us will experience the pain of a broken heart and glimpse the abyss of hopelessness more than once during our life. The wisdom Ron shares in this book reveals practical steps that lead from the valley of the shadow of death to the sundrenched slopes of hope. I saw my own heartbreak in part two and my own life is brighter because of this book. Yours will be too.

—**Ken Davis**, author, professional speaker, president of Dynamic Communicators

Part of my calling as a pastor is to give hope to hurting people. But hope can be fragile, and holding on to it can be a real struggle. Ron Hutchcraft knows this battle well. Like so many of us, he also has fought to hold on to hope during dark, painful times. That's the reason *Hope When Your Heart Is Breaking* is such a blessing and a treasure. Thank you, Ron, for showing us the way to keep hope alive. What a gift!

—**Dr. Crawford W. Loritts, Jr.**, author, speaker, radio host, and senior pastor, Fellowship Bible Church

There are many takeaways in this book...but the following three are my favorites. They will prove helpful to everyone who embraces them: *I will not deny my pain; I will not be defined by my loss; I will rely on an unseen but certain Hope beyond the hurt.* Thank you, Ron. These are an enormous help.

—**Robert Wolgemuth**, bestselling author

Ron Hutchcraft is a faithful steward of pain. This book is not simply good advice; it's life-tested, rock-solid truth you can rely on. There is no broken part of your life God does not see. Trust Him with your broken pieces. Reading Ron's book will provide hope and light in the darkness.

—**Chris Fabry**, host of *Chris Fabry Live*,
author of *A Piece of the Moon*

Has there ever been a time when you didn't have the answers to life's deep questions during a great loss in your life? How do you respond in times of uncertainty and overwhelming fear? What do you do when your whole world collapses around you and you feel so alone? Ron so tenderly and genuinely communicates a life lesson learned from the One who created him. Once you pick this book up, you will not want to put it down until you receive all from God's conversation with Ron.

—**Huron Claus**, president, CHIEF Inc.
(Christian Hope Indian Eskimo Fellowship)

Ron's words create poignant, transforming pictures in our minds, drawing us to a higher place. Better than cloud-chasing hope, Scripture's truths can be grasped, lifting us to that place. Not cotton candy—sweet for only a moment—but truths that provide strength through the valley. I've been through that valley myself. I commend Ron's words to you, because they are our Lord's words. Hope guaranteed.

—**Miriam Neff**, founder and president of Widow
Connection, author, counselor, and speaker

I have had a half-century friendship with the man of God who wrote this greatly needed and relevant book. With suffering out of control in the world today, this message is not optional. If you are in a hurry, start with the last chapter—"The Only Safe Place."

—**George Verwer, DD**, founder of Operation Mobilization

This side of glory, we will have pain, loss, and heartache. But we also have something else—hope. Ron reminds us of God's Word: *Hope* never fails. It's what gets you through the night, past the pain, and into the center of His love. Drink in these pages and be reminded of the priceless constancy of the gift of hope.

—**Janet Parshall**, nationally syndicated talk show host, author

Ron opens up his heart to honestly reveal both the pain and the peace, the grief and the goodness, and the emptiness and the fullness of Christ's presence in the middle of a storm. This book will be transformational to anyone searching for a heartfelt, honest approach to a sudden loss.

—**Joe Battaglia**, broadcaster, author of *Make America Good Again*, president of Renaissance Communications

Most of us don't stop to consider how vital, how essential hope is—until we feel it starting to slip away. Ron Hutchcraft has learned how to fight for hope and where to look when hope is hard to see. He has given all of us a great gift here. This book will breathe fresh hope into even the most discouraged heart.

—**Bob Lepine**, cohost, *FamilyLife Today*

Every time I hear or read Ron Hutchcraft, I know Jesus is at the center of the message. He is always pointing us to Jesus. This book is another great example of this. You'll be inspired to anchor your faith in Jesus through every storm.

—**Ted Cunningham**, pastor, Woodland Hills Family Church, author of *Fun Loving You*

I think the integrity of Ron Hutchcraft and the timeliness of this book is no coincidence. If there's one thing we need right now, it's hope. Thank you for leading us to the only one who can give us hope, Jesus.

—**Grant Skeldon**, Next Gen director for Q, author of *The Passion Generation*

Ron Hutchcraft acknowledges the hardship of pain and suffering while also encouraging that despair does not have to be the end of the story. Because of the gospel, we do not have to succumb to despair, but we have the authority in Jesus to walk in hope that cannot be shaken.

—**Emma Mae Jenkins**, author of *Be Loved* and *All Caps YOU*, Gen Z social media influencer/speaker

HOPE
When Your
Heart Is
Breaking

RON HUTCHCRAFT

HARVEST HOUSE PUBLISHERS
EUGENE, OREGON

Cover design by Kyler Dougherty

Cover photo © darkbird77, mom noi, Sjo, Tolga TEZCAN / Gettyimages

Interior design by KUHN Design Group

Published in association with the literary agency of WordServe Literary Group, Ltd., www.word serveliterary.com.

For bulk, special sales, or ministry purchases, please call 1-800-547-8979.
E-mail: Customerservice@hhpbooks. com

Hope When Your Heart Is Breaking
Copyright © 2021 by Ronald P. Hutchcraft
Published by Harvest House Publishers
Eugene, Oregon 97408
www. harvesthousepublishers.com

ISBN 978-0-7369-8141-5 (pbk.)
ISBN 978-0-7369-8142-2 (eBook)

Library of Congress Cataloging-in-Publication Data
Names: Hutchcraft, Ronald, author.
Title: Hope when your heart is breaking : finding God's presence in your pain / Ronald Hutchcraft.
Description: Eugene, Oregon : Harvest House Publishers, 2021. | Summary:
"Ron Hutchcraft has walked that dark valley called grief. From it, he offers Hope When Your Heart Is Breaking-a practical pathway through the pain, and the choices that lead to healing and hope"-- Provided by publisher.
Identifiers: LCCN 2020029034 (print) | LCCN 2020029035 (ebook) | ISBN 9780736981415 (trade paperback) | ISBN 9780736981422 (ebook)
Subjects: LCSH: Grief--Religious aspects--Christianity. |
Bereavement--Religious aspects--Christianity. | Consolation. |
Hope--Religious aspects--Christianity.
Classification: LCC BV4909 .H875 2021 (print) | LCC BV4909 (ebook) | DDC 248.8/6--dc23
LC record available at https://lccn.loc.gov/2020029034
LC ebook record available at https://lccn.loc.gov/2020029035

To the life and memory of my Karen,
the love of my life.

———◦◦◦———

I am forever grateful for her enduring love. Her undying loyalty. Her life-changing wisdom. Her belief in me, when I deserved it and when I didn't. Her uncompromised honesty. Her delightful unpredictability. Her profound walk with God. And her incomparable laugh. She was so much more than my "better half." She made my half so much better than it ever could have been without her. Only heaven will show how much of what I have done and what I have become is because God gave me Karen.

My "beyond words" gratitude goes to our three children—Lisa, Doug and Brad—and to Rick, Anna, and Sara, the amazing people they married; and to my selfless sister-in-law, Valerie. Their love and support and encouragement have been the difference over and over again.

CONTENTS

—⚬⚬⚬—

BEFORE YOU BEGIN

by Joni Eareckson Tada

Y ou've been through it. A whirlwind of devastations that rip through your sanity or a haunting depression that lingers like a low-grade fever. Or it could be the insistent nagging of chronic pain. It happened to me the other night. As a quadriplegic, my husband, Ken, must position me on my side with pillows so I can sleep. Sensing pain on the rise and knowing I would not be able to adjust myself, my breathing got shorter. "Pray that I won't lose hope," I whispered to Ken.

I am always amazed at how often our hope is put to the test. A festering sore, a pinched nerve, the slow ticking of the clock, or the terror of feeling all alone in your struggle. Like me when paralysis and pain nearly overwhelm me. It drains almost all hope out of my heart.

Almost.

That's the story of Ron Hutchcraft. When I first read the book you hold in your hands, I was stunned. I've never seen Ron without a winsome, confident smile and a bounce in his step. His faith is strong, his calling is clear, and I don't think the man ever misses an opportunity to tell others about Jesus. Ron is the picture of assurance, strength, and resolve. But then the untimely death of his beloved life-partner almost took him out of the battle. *Almost.*

It is why I found *Hope When Your Heart Is Breaking* to be such a blessing. Ron invites the reader into the innermost chamber in his heart, a place not many strong men even speak of, let alone reveal. It's a broken place, and when he describes his pain, you feel as though he is limping on shards of glass.

But it is what makes this book believable. Authentic. Convincing. So when this seasoned student of God's Word invites you to take the same path that led him up and out of emptiness, you listen. You follow his directives. You trust his guidance through the hope-filled pages of Scripture.

Hope When Your Heart Is Breaking is your husky, bravehearted guide through dark valleys into the fresh air of biblical hope. Its pages may be splattered with pain, but you will find on them eternal principles that will be a light for your path. Do not fear if your world is almost splitting apart at the seams. Just take your favorite coffee to your easy chair, get started reading, and let Ron bring you back from the edge of *almost.*

Joni Eareckson Tada
Joni and Friends International
Disability Center, 2020

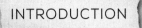

HOPE AS REAL AS THE HURT

I t was, as the saying goes, "a dark and stormy night."

We had just finished an event on a Native American reservation, led by a team of inspiring Native young people. All night those storm clouds had hovered around the basketball court but mercifully held off during the event.

Once we were safely in the church basement where we were staying, those angry skies blew their top. After a lightning strike that sounded as though it was moving in, we were suddenly plunged into pitch-black darkness. The only thing worse than the lightning was the girls' screaming.

We couldn't see anybody or anything, and with a nasty storm sounding off outside—well, it was creepy. Eerily quiet for a basement full of young people.

After a few nervous minutes in the dark, someone found a candle.

"Anybody got a match?" Yup. One precious candle and one priceless match. I cannot begin to tell you the change in that room when that little flame flickered to life.

It wasn't much. Just a little light. But it changed everything.

In our personal dark times—and we all have them—that little flame has a name. It's called hope. And it changes everything.

But that flame can be fragile too. It can be extinguished all too easily—and leave us alone and afraid in the dark again.

Hope has been taking a beating in our generation. The late United States senator John McCain said, not long before his passing: "The world is in greater turmoil than at any other time in my lifetime."

The future we might have been confident of not so long ago now is looking increasingly uncertain. You can feel the unease. The anxiety. Even anger.

As we absorb each day's breaking news, it seems as if there's a tsunami of mega-problems that overwhelms our answers. Our headlines are dominated by the unpredictable. The unthinkable. Our politics are chaotic and toxic, the financial world is vulnerable, and our safe places aren't safe anymore.

It's increasingly disturbing to contemplate the kind of world our children and grandchildren will have to navigate without a map. One friend summed it up pretty well: "It just seems like nothing is working."

Again and again, we're hit with how quickly the flame of hope can go out. A storm...a quake...a pandemic...an accident...a breakup...a job loss...a financial disaster...bad news from the doctor. Life's unexpected losses keep reminding us how insecure our security is. How not in control we really are. How quickly our "go to" person or thing can be gone.

It turns out, hope is more fragile than we knew. People and anchors who secure our lives are more "losable" than we realized.

I know. One night the amazing woman I had loved since I was 19 was by my side at our grandson's graduation. The next afternoon, she was gone.

Whenever I would come home from work or a trip, I'd head for our great room and immediately look over at Karen's blue recliner. I could see her beautiful gray hair—her "crown of glory"—as I came through the door. I would know my baby was there and the world was okay.

But that day, the blue chair was empty. And I would never see her crown of glory there again.

The loss was incalculable. It touched every part of my life and my future. Suddenly my personal world was turned upside down. The light had gone out.

Oh, how I needed hope. And, oh, what I have learned about what hope is and what it isn't. By the nature of my people-helping life's work, I've walked with many through their dark valleys—jobs, marriage, divorce, children, faith, failure, heartbreak—and yes, grief. And I've learned about hope what only real life can teach.

Grief isn't just about losing a person you love. That's certainly the big one, but definitely not the only one. Loss comes in many forms. Losing your marriage. Losing your dream. Losing your health. Losing your job...your income...your retirement. Losing a child emotionally or spiritually. Losing a treasured relationship or the future you had planned. Or the quiet grieving of what was lost—or taken from you—in the past.

Wherever there's loss, there's grieving. And wherever there's grieving, there are choices. Some lead to hope and healing. Some lead to more hurt and more grief.

In J.R.R. Tolkien's trilogy, The Lord of the Rings, two characters are discussing the looming invasion by sinister forces that threatens their lives in Middle-earth.

I was struck by how aptly it describes our human experience when a dark season of loss upends our life.

"I wish it need not have happened in my time," said Frodo.

"So do I," said Gandalf, "and so do all who live to see such times. But that is not for them to decide. All we have to decide is what to do with the time that is given us."

Indeed, we have no choice about the loss we are grieving. I had no choice about my Karen's passing. But my future would not be decided primarily by her death, but by what I did with that heartrending loss.

So if you were to ask me what this book is about, and I had to do it in four words, I'd say loss...grief...choices...hope. Not "hope" the concept. But "hope" the experience. Hope the choice.

For hope to overcome despair in life's dark valleys, it has to be something more than the syrupy, unanchored variety usually offered to us. More than the Wikipedia definition of hope as "an optimistic attitude of mind based on expectation of positive outcomes."

The hope needs to be as real as the hurt. As strong as the grief. As compelling as the fear. As powerful as the pull to give up.

So what's in these pages is not philosophical. It's deeply, deeply personal. Down-to-earth practical. And real.

I've seen hope that failed to deliver, like a light that goes out when you're in the dark. But I've also seen the kind of hope that keeps lighting up the darkness.

Defiant hope.

Hope that finds the healing presence of God Himself in the midst of the rubble. A hope that shakes its fist at despair and fear and shouts, "No! You can't have me!"

That's worth writing about. And, I hope, worth reading about.

PART ONE

THE FLAG OVER THE RUBBLE

CHAPTER 1

EMOTIONAL OXYGEN

But I know somehow that only when it is
dark enough can you see the stars.

D<small>R</small>. M<small>ARTIN</small> L<small>UTHER</small> K<small>ING</small>

C ode Blue."

The announcement that summons all available medical personnel to a life-or-death emergency. Except this day it was the person I loved more than anyone in the world.

My wife's procedure that day was really just a test. A heart catheterization to check her arteries. I was passing the waiting room time tackling a couple of items on my to-do list.

Then that announcement. "Code Blue." Never occurred to me that it could be my Karen.

It was. I knew as soon as the waiting room door opened and I saw the look on the doctor's face. Later, I would learn that her lungs had suddenly been overwhelmed with seven and a half liters of fluid. She was drowning, and no one knew. Until the doctor said, "I don't like how her color has changed."

My mind went into overdrive, flooded with what this could mean. Had I held the love of my life for the last time? I've done my whole life with her. How can I do the rest of it without her?

I was gasping for emotional oxygen. I was desperate for hope.

GASPING FOR AIR

In medical terms, they "bagged" my wife that Code Blue day— using a respirator bag to push life-saving oxygen into her lungs. To save her from literally drowning right in front of them.

Drowning is a pretty fair description of how it feels emotionally when one of life's sledgehammers hits. In those moments that seem to knock the breath out of us.

The death of a marriage. The diagnosis that could mean either a death sentence or a life sentence of pain. The life-scarring choice made by your prodigal son or daughter. The caregiving that is pushing you to the limit. The "your mother and I are getting a divorce" that shatters your security.

The crisis of hope can come from the painful past that pursues you wherever you go. The "we don't need you anymore" from the company you've given so much to. The verdict that you won't be able to have children. The devastating failure.

For most of us, there has been—or there will be—that crushing time when we are desperate for a life preserver. We are drowning.

Like the day when Laura learned her husband was suddenly arrested for sexual crimes with underage girls. Or the day Greg and Tammy were informed that their five-year-old daughter had terminal leukemia. Or when the one man Beth had learned to trust—her mother's boyfriend—sexually assaulted her.

Or that awful day when the love of my life was gone in one

life-shattering moment. God had graciously given her back to me ten years ago after her Code Blue crisis. But now, the woman I adored, the only person I've done every day of my adult life with, was suddenly gone.

Most of us know the feeling on some level. A loss that levels us. A storm that obscures the sun we've always navigated by. A blow that leaves us feeling lost on a road with no map.

Gasping for air. Grasping for a life preserver.

WIMPY HOPE

Hope really is the emotional oxygen that keeps us going. "Things will get better." "It doesn't have to be the way it's always been." "Something good is about to happen."

The dictionary variously defines *hope* as "a feeling of expectation" or "a desire for certain things to happen." Or "grounds for believing something good may happen" and "intending, if possible, to do something."

Nice. But not enough. Not for the 7.5 lifequakes. The Category 5 storms. We need more than a "feeling," a "desire," or "an optimistic attitude." The blows are heavy. A lot of "hope" is Hope Lite. Too wimpy to bring us back when we can barely breathe. And no match for the moments that seem to shatter hope.

Hope has to be more than "when you wish upon a star." Or crossing your fingers. Or just quoting inspiring slogans from a motivational speaker.

We need something more muscular, more durable, more authentic.

There is hope like that. I know. It's the air I'm breathing right now. That's sustaining each of the shell-shocked people I mentioned earlier.

But it doesn't come from your circumstances. It comes from your choices.

THE FLAG IN THE RUBBLE

"You should turn on the TV. An airplane just crashed into one of the World Trade Center towers."

A family member called to alert me. Who could have possibly known the unspeakable tragedy we were about to see unfold that fateful September day?

We'd been to the top of the World Trade Center many times. I knew someone who worked in an office there. To see those seemingly indestructible towers crumble to dust before our eyes—there are no words for it.

News anchors usually report the news dispassionately. Not on September 11, 2001. Like most of us, they could not conceal their disbelief and grief.

Suddenly, we were feeling something Americans were not used to feeling. Vulnerable. Our hallowed space between two protecting oceans had been brutally invaded. And we would never feel the same kind of safe again.

For a few hours, there were some hopes that a massive rescue effort could still save many lives. Those hopes were short-lived. An evacuation order was issued to all firefighters searching in the rubble. By late that afternoon, hope was hard to find.

And then, the flag.

Three weary firefighters. The dusty flag they had recovered from a boat in the harbor. They couldn't possibly have known what the simple act of raising that flag over that heartbreaking pile of rubble would mean.

It remains the most iconic image of a generation's darkest day.

Or, as *USA Today* said in their next edition, "It was hope on a day when it seemed that all hope was gone."

It flew above the wreckage of a heart-shattering day. And seemed to say against a backdrop that appeared to represent only despair: "It isn't over, folks. There's hope."

Yes.

Defiant hope!

THE COUNTERPUNCH

Truck drivers see it all the time. I've seen it a few times when we've needed to drive through the night.

It comes about the time you've opened the window on a frigid night. And you've turned to the most annoying radio station you can find. Because the night is getting long, and your eyelids are staying a little too long in the down position. To top it off, it seems like the dark has gotten darker as morning approaches.

Suddenly, there it is. A dim but distinct glow in the eastern sky. Oh, it's still really dark, for the most part. But the glow will grow. And as it brightens, so does the horizon. Still dark, but something's happening out there.

And you know the long night isn't going to be forever. There's light on the edges. And the light is pushing aside a wider and higher swath of that numbing darkness.

Ultimately, there's that glorious moment when, preceded by glowing clouds, the sun teases the horizon. And in minutes, the darkness has lost. The sun has won. And the first light that had only brightened the horizon soon illuminates the whole landscape.

That's my picture of hope. That's why, on many mornings, I stand at the window, watching the sunrise.

Every sunset in my lifetime has been followed by a sunrise. Without fail.

By virtue of the people-helping work I do, I've walked with many

through their darkest nights. And beginning the day I lost my wife—
my baby—I believe I have been walking through mine.

And I'm ready to venture a real-life definition of *hope*. Of *defiant
hope*:

> *Hope is a buoyant confidence, acknowledging the hurt,*
> *but anchored in an unseen but certain reality.*

No, not wishful thinking. No, not inspirational slogans. Not escap-
ist denial.

But a confidence that squarely faces the loss and the unanswered
questions, yet chooses to not be defined by them.

Rather, to trust life's Grand Weaver to make something meaning-
ful—even beautiful—out of these dark threads.

Hope requires choices that defy the seeming hopelessness you may
feel. In the pages ahead, we will explore five of life's hope robbers, along
with the choices that offer short-term relief—but long term, only more
pain. More importantly, we will discover the choices that will help us
breathe the life-restoring oxygen of hope.

Choices that don't deny but do defy the pain of your past. The grief
in your heart. The wilderness that surrounds you. The danger in our
world. The seemingly unfixable brokenness of your marriage. The bitterness that seethes in your soul. The failure that has made you not
want to get up. The sad story that has been much of your life. The person or situation that seems like it will never change.

There is a way to make it through the darkest night. There is a way
to raise a flag of hope over the rubble.

It's called *defiant hope*!

CHAPTER 2

SINKING SHIP, UNSINKABLE YOU

When you're at the end of your rope,
tie a knot and hang on.

THEODORE ROOSEVELT

I t's nice to have a friend who has a sailboat. Or, as my friend Dave used to say, "A hole in the water into which you pour money."

His boat wasn't just for him and his family—it was for the enjoyment of his friends too. Our family has some rich memories of hours spent with him on Long Island Sound. My wife and I celebrated a wedding anniversary by spending the night on that boat. Not at sea, of course. Just rocked to sleep by the water as the boat sat anchored in the harbor.

Dave decided to do a night on the boat too. During a hurricane! He didn't invite me, and that was fine. His report on his rock-and-roll night: "Man, the storm blew me all around, but it didn't blow me away. Thanks to the anchor."

I think that's what my dad wanted the night before his open-heart surgery. His anchor.

That procedure was relatively new when the doctors decided it was my father's best option. Needless to say, he had plenty of justifiable anxiety as the day of that massive surgery neared.

He asked me to read something to him from the Bible. "Could you read the Twenty-third Psalm?" Good choice. That particular section of the Bible has been a source of hope—and an anchor—for countless people at critical moments.

So, as he lay in his hospital bed, eyes closed to focus, I started reading the familiar words of King David: "The Lord is my shepherd; I shall not want. He makes me to lie down in green pastures; He leads me beside the still waters. He restores my soul" (Psalm 23:1-3 nkjv).

I think it was the words that followed that he most wanted to hear: "Though I walk through the valley of the shadow of death, I will fear no evil, for You are with me…Surely goodness and mercy shall follow me all the days of my life, and I shall dwell in the house of the Lord forever" (Psalm 23:4,6).

Those words were, for me, at once comforting to hear and hard to hear. Dad seemed at peace when I finished reading. There was hope in that ancient Shepherd Psalm.

He never regained consciousness after that surgery. He lingered for a month, but then he was gone. In a medical sense, my dad "died" that day in May. Biblically, he relocated. To "the house of the Lord forever."

MY CATEGORY 5 STORM

It was tough losing my dad. It was devastating losing my wife— this was the storm that rocked me to the core and tested everything I'd ever held onto.

Years ago, I asked our friend Nancy how she was doing since her accomplished husband had died. It was the first time I'd seen her since that happened. I've never forgotten what she told me: "Ron, this is the final exam. And you can't cram for it. You're either ready or you're not."

It really is the final exam. And the greatest hope crisis of my life.

No Karen.

For anyone who's known us, "Ron and Karen" has been one word. Hard to say one name without the other. And that's how our life has been since we first fell in love. A loving, powerful partnership on so many levels.

Suddenly, it's just Ron.

I was going to need everything I'd ever known, ever heard, ever seen, ever learned about hope. And more.

Like my dad, and like millions of others throughout the ages, my heart landed in the only harbor where I could be safe. With the only anchor that could hold me in a storm this merciless.

I went to the world's best-selling book. The Bible.

And there really is hope there. Not "up in the clouds" hope. But anchored hope. Once again, my life-learned definition:

> *Hope is a buoyant confidence, acknowledging the hurt,*
> *but anchored in an unseen but certain reality.*

A crisis of hope is usually triggered by losing one of our life anchors. A person, financial security, health, job, marriage, independence, or just our confidence in the future.

But in the face of loss, hope is *buoyant confidence.* You can push a cork under the water, but as soon as you let go, it's coming back up! You can sink it, but you can't drown it.

Defiant hope doesn't mean you don't go down. It means you don't

stay down. Whether your storm is from grief or failure, abuse or aban-
donment, disease or divorce, you may very well go under when it first hits.
The question is whether you *stay* down. You didn't have a choice
about the hit or the hurt. But you do have a choice about the hope.

DROPPING ANCHOR

On the most heart-shattering day of my life, I was desperate for
hope on two levels.

First, where the love of my life was now.

I chose to drop anchor in Scripture:

> …away from the body and at home with the Lord
> (2 Corinthians 5:8).

> [Jesus answered,] "Do not let your hearts be troubled…My
> Father's house has many rooms…I am going there to pre-
> pare a place for you…I will come back and take you to be
> with me" (John 14:1-3).

> [Jesus said,] "I am the resurrection and the life. The one
> who believes in me will live, even though they die" (John
> 11:25).

Since, according to contemporary historians, Jesus rose from the
dead, I'm thinking what He says about death is the final word.

So, my wounded heart took great comfort that fateful May day
from this unseen but certain reality. To say Karen had "died" was woe-
fully inadequate. The reality is, "She went to be with Jesus."

That made buoyant confidence possible on the day I was sinking fast.

But there's a problem. Karen's with Jesus. I'm still here. Without her.
I've only done life *with* her. The hole she's left is huge.

She's the only person who's been on the journey with me through every joy, every sorrow, every battle. She knew all the people I know, shared the same memories that I cherish, laughed with me, cried with me, prayed with me, advised me through it all. She's *irreplaceable*! So how do I do life *without* her?

My sobbing that day and since isn't for where my baby is. It's for the unfillable hole in my heart and my life. For the hole in the lives of our family. It's the minor-key score that plays softly in the background as I do my days.

Looking up, my hope for Karen—and for an ultimate reunion—was secure. But looking ahead to all those days without her wisdom and love—that's where I was gasping for the emotional oxygen of hope.

Once again, I dropped anchor in Scripture verses that have sustained countless people in their times of loss and fear:

> My grace is sufficient for you (2 Corinthians 12:9).
>
> Your strength will equal your days (Deuteronomy 33:25).
>
> Be strong in the grace that is in Christ Jesus (2 Timothy 2:1).
>
> I can do all things through Christ who strengthens me (Philippians 4:13 NKJV).

It seemed like the Shepherd of my dad's Twenty-third Psalm was saying to me, "We'll do this together, one day at a time. And you'll be okay."

I planted my feet on the rock of those unseen but certain realities. Rather than in the mire of my raw and shifting emotions.

More than that, I found in the Bible's time-tested wisdom two defining realities for making the choices that replace despair and fear with hope. While each of the battles against life's hope killers requires a different kind of choice, they all rest on two foundations—two rocks to stand on.

DAFFODILS IN THE SNOW

It had been a bipolar winter. Enough warm days to make the buds think it was warm enough to pop out on the trees. But cold enough to make them sorry.

Which led to one of the more unusual pictures I've ever taken. There, on the south side of our house, were those bright yellow daffodils. Poking through the snow.

Now, surveying the frigid white landscape that day, you wouldn't be thinking "Spring!" Except for that yellow harbinger, spring was "an unseen but certain reality." Not yet. But for sure.

Hope that defies despair is anchored in a reality that is not yet, but for sure. If you make the choices that appropriate hope.

Those choices require looking at a "hopeless" situation through the wide-angle lens provided by a divine perspective on it. In my darkest hour, in many other hope-robbing moments, I could choose hope based on two greater realities.

The Plan

Some days, you have to watch the news for a long time before there's any good news. I think it was on one of those days when the more I watched, the more depressing it got.

From somewhere deep in my memory, a statement from the Bible suddenly popped up. I quickly turned to that passage to read it in light of news that seemed to say, "The sky is falling!"

First, it asked an amazingly pertinent question: "When the foundations are being destroyed, what can the righteous do?" (Psalm 11:3).

Good question!

At first, the answer didn't seem like an answer: "The LORD is in his holy temple; the LORD is on his heavenly throne" (Psalm 11:4).

Right. So? Then I got it. Everything's moving—except God on His throne. He's in charge, not presidents or senators or generals or corporations or terrorists. So if He's your security, your security hasn't moved. Can't move.

That becomes more than a Bible verse on the day you feel like you've lost everything. It is your *anchor.* The only thing that keeps your boat from sinking. Blown around, yes. Blown away, no.

And that unchallengeable God is doing something in my life at that moment that is so much bigger than what I can see or feel.

His guarantee says:

> All things work together for good to those who love God (Romans 8:28 NKJV).

> I know the plans I have for you...plans to prosper you and not to harm you, plans to give you hope and a future (Jeremiah 29:11).

Somewhere, buried beneath my grief and my agonized questions is a Plan. It's unseen right now. But it's certain.

So, standing there in a mountain of hurt, there is a "daffodil in the snow." *There's something bigger going on than the thing I can see!*

Maybe if I focus on that, I can make the choices that will redeem this pain rather than deepen it.

The Provision

It's helpful to know there's a plan, a purpose in this pain. But how do I make it through the uncharted wilderness I just entered? Knowing there's a plan doesn't help my broken heart.

That's where another divine guarantee gives me hope that the unbearable will, in fact, be bearable. And the undoable will be doable.

It's recorded in the biblical writings of Paul, the man most responsible for the spread of the Jesus story in the first century. This man, whose itinerant work required enormous physical stamina, had a tormenting physical condition he described as his "thorn in the flesh." At the point of despair, he cried out again and again for God to take it from him.

He got a different answer: "But He said to me, 'My grace is sufficient for you, for my power is made perfect in weakness'" (2 Corinthians 12:9).

And as a grace-carried messenger, Paul would proclaim: "When I am weak, then I am strong" (2 Corinthians 9:10).

All I can tell you is that what he said is true. I'm living it in these sometimes sad, sometimes lonely, sometimes challenging days of my life.

It's like adrenaline. When there's a crisis, our body suddenly unleashes this glandular rush called adrenaline. And the stories are incredible of what people could suddenly do with that injection of uncommon strength. A person can lift what they otherwise could never lift.

Grace is spiritual adrenaline.

If I look at what I can handle when a hope robber hits, I'll sink or give up. Unless I go with the grace factor. Each day it's as if God makes another grace delivery. And no matter the burden, it is, as He promised, "sufficient."

There's a reason they call grace amazing.

WHY HOPE IS DEFIANT

I love the dictionary definition of *defiant*: "a disposition to challenge, resist, fight; boldly resisting, challenging."

Without the choices that unleash hope, we are defined by our loss, our wounds, our fear. So there's a decision to be made.

To challenge hopelessness. To resist. Not to deny the pain, but to refuse to be defined by the pain.

Hope is usually not our default response when we're hit hard or hurt deeply. Instead, there's depression. Anger or anxiety. Paralysis or pity. Lashing out or dropping out. Giving out or giving up. So hope has to be a defiant choice.

Because…

Hope is a fist in the face of surrender.

When a staggering blow, a crushing loss hits, defiant hope chooses to respond with three courageous affirmations:

- *I will not deny my pain.*

- *But I will not be defined by my loss.*

- *And I will rely on an unseen but certain Hope beyond the hurt.*

There are defiant hope choices I've seen wounded people make that have taken their life higher than ever before. Choices that have redeemed their brokenness and recycled it into hope for other broken people. We will explore what those choices look like in the face of five powerful, but not invincible, hope robbers.

Five of life's hope-robbing storms. And the hope-filled choices that defy and defeat despair. As well as the life-changing outcomes that recycle a loss into a stronger, more resilient you than ever before.

Right now, I continue to battle the storm of grief head-on, doing my best to make the choices that unleash hope.

I'm like my sailing friend Dave, hanging on inside his boat as the hurricane winds rocked his world. Doing okay "thanks to the anchor."

When caring friends ask me how I'm doing, the short answer comes down to three words: The Anchor holds.

It really does.

CHAPTER 3

YOUR LAST CARD— HOPE IS A CHOICE

Where there's hope, there's life. It fills us with fresh courage and makes us strong again.

ANNE FRANK

I have asked groups of young people—even business leaders—to do it. Suddenly, I was doing it. For real.

After giving everyone in the room four 3 x 5 cards, I've asked them to write on those cards the four most important things or people in their life. Then I've asked them to make a choice.

"A tragedy hits your life—and you're going to lose one of the most important things in your life. Except, unlike real life, you choose which one you lose. Drop that card on the floor." I get some weird looks, but soon cards are dropping.

It starts to get ugly when I ask them to make that same kind of choice again. And then, "With just the two most important things in your life left, a tragedy is going to take one of them. You can keep one, but you have to drop one."

For some people, it's virtually impossible to make that choice. But eventually, everyone is down to one card. Now comes the *question*.

"You now are holding in your hand a card that represents the most important thing or person in your life. Here's the important question to ask: 'Is it something I can *lose*?'"

That day in May, when the love of my life was suddenly gone, I felt like it was my "two-card" moment. My next-to-the-last card was taken from my hand. I was, in a moment, left with one card. It was my #1.

The card I lost was the woman I couldn't imagine living without. But the card I had left was what I would have chosen as my last card.

The only treasure I cannot lose.

I would have written on my last card, "My personal love relationship with Jesus Christ." Not Jesus the religion. Jesus the *relationship*. It is my one certain reality. The anchor for my hope—no matter what cards I may lose.

It is hope with a written guarantee—from God Himself, as recorded in His Book:

> Neither death nor life, neither angels nor demons, neither the present nor the future, nor any powers, neither height nor depth, nor anything else in all creation, will be able to separate us from the love of God that is in Christ Jesus our Lord (Romans 8:38-39).

Disease-proof. Divorce-proof. Disaster-proof. *Death*-proof.

All other hopes have one disqualifying weakness: They're "loseable." A truth that hit me like a truck when "my baby," who had been so alive just the night before, was suddenly gone from my arms.

I was painfully vulnerable. Unspeakably sad. But I was safe.

STRONGER THAN THE ROBBERS

The hope robbers we will face in the pages ahead are strong. The ripping and tearing of grief. The doubt and discouragement of pain and suffering. The sting of failure—in your work, in relationships, in your finances, in your education, in your dream. The heartbreak and self-doubt of a broken love, a breaking or broken marriage. The lifequake of broken health. The relentless dark cloud of the wounds and pain of your past.

Hope must be strong to fight back after knockout punches like these. And in order for hope to be strong, it has to be "unlosable." The anchor has to be stronger than the storm.

That's why so many—for so long—have anchored their hope to Jesus. The uniqueness of the hope He offers is described by one of the men who knew Him best, His disciple Simon Peter: "He has given us new birth into a *living hope* through the resurrection of Jesus Christ from the dead" (1 Peter 1:3, emphasis added).

This hope is not a program, not a pill, not a religion or a belief. It's a *Person*.

He is the only Person in human history who conquered what has conquered every other person who's ever lived: death. Brutally crucified by Rome's professional executioners. Buried in a tomb sealed with a massive stone and guarded by soldiers who were charged by the governor to "make it as secure as you can." They did. But the Man in the tomb was unstoppable.

So hope has a name. His name is Jesus. He is *living* hope. The unseen but certain hope that energizes a buoyant confidence, defying life's deepest hurts and darkest valleys.

Does the hope erase the pain, the grief? No. It envelops it. It is the greater counterweight on the other side of the scale. For me, the sadness and loneliness are always lurking in the background. But the

hope—along with its by-products of joy and peace—are the promi-
nent, major-chord melody playing loudly in the foreground.

TWO BROKEN MEN

All I remember is a chaotic night in our little apartment on the south
side of Chicago. My parents whisked my baby brother out the door,
wrapped in a blanket. My grandmother whisked me off to her house.
I never saw my baby brother, Steven, again. The doctors weren't
even sure what he died from.

My daddy seemed to cry all the time. He was a broken man. Knowing what I know now, I would say he was inconsolable. Without hope.

For some reason, he thought it would be a good idea to take his
remaining son to church. I had never been in a church, let alone heard
about Jesus. My dad would stay in the car out front in his machinist's
clothes, reading his paper and smoking his cigarette.

One Sunday, I ran to the car and announced, "Daddy, I asked Jesus
into my heart this morning." I'm pretty sure he had no idea what I was
talking about.

Until he ventured inside that church one day. Where he learned
what I had learned about Jesus. That He had come from heaven to
become, in the Bible's words, "a Man of sorrows and acquainted with
grief" (Isaiah 53:3 NKJV). And that this Jesus bore our sins "in his body
on the cross" (1 Peter 2:24), making it possible for the sins of a lifetime
to be forgiven and erased from God's book.

One day, my broken daddy decided to put his life in the hands of
the Savior who was broken for him. He was never the same. I got a new
daddy. My mom got a new husband. And while he never got over the
death of my brother, he was known by everyone for his smile, his joy,
and his encouragement.

It was a buoyant confidence that acknowledged the loss, but was anchored to an invisible but certain reality.

The broken man in my wife's family was her grandfather Bill. Bill had a lucrative and successful career as a telegrapher—until his addiction to alcohol and drugs became his slave master. Robbing a post office to get some drug money sent him to federal prison. At one point, he had become so desperate for cocaine that he dug the gold fillings out of his teeth to get some money.

His life was a hopeless wreck that night when he was walking along downtown Chicago's State Street, wearing pieces of cardboard for shoes. He was on his way to Lake Michigan to end his life.

That's when he heard the familiar song coming out of the rescue mission he was passing. It was a hymn his mother had sung to him. When he went inside, a mission worker began to tell him about this Jesus who made people into, as the Bible says, a "new creation" in Christ (2 Corinthians 5:17).

When the mission worker began to quote an amazing Bible verse, Bill finished it. Again, seeds planted by a praying mother a long time ago…

> God so loved the world that he gave his one and only Son, that whoever believes in him shall not perish but have eternal life (John 3:16).

That night, on the way to take his life, Bill gave his life to Jesus. Like my dad, he was never the same. He often said, "I am not a reformed man. I am a *transformed* man!"

Traveling across the country to share the Hope he had found, this broken man became a source of hope for many other hope-starved people.

For my broken dad, for my wife's suicidal grandfather, only one kind of hope could have saved them. A *living* hope. Jesus. The Resurrection

Man. They were too far gone for any answer other than a transcendent hope, with healing, redeeming power. Resurrection power.

THE ELEVATOR TO THE TOP

My friend was about to try one of this world's most dangerous sports—driving in Manhattan. Having driven there many times in the crunch of speeding taxis, truck-blocked streets, bullying buses, and oblivious pedestrian posses, I had some advice: "Drive safe…and die." I was joking. Sort of.

The streets of New York are, to some, exciting. To others, terrifying. If you're new to the Big Apple, it's stressful, overwhelming, and occasionally dangerous.

But there's more to New York than the streets. There's the view. Take one of those elevators that rocket to the top of one of the city's skyscrapers. The view from the observation deck is unforgettable. There's the Statue of Liberty and the ships plying the harbor. From another window, you can see the city's lineup of magnificent bridges. Oh, and there's Central Park, that beautiful sea of green in the middle of a jungle of concrete.

It's crazy on the street. But it all looks different from the top floor.

When Jesus came, He walked the cold and stressful streets of our world. He lived the pain of betrayal, of injustice, of awful loneliness, of hellish temptation, of violent death.

But when He died on that cross and vacated that sealed tomb, He gave us an elevator to the top floor. A perspective on the pain and unfairness and grieving of our life.

It's called "eternity."

Our embattled lives on earth are not all there is. This is the opening act. The warm-up. The beginning. This is Hotel Earth. Not home.

Years ago, a Ghanaian diplomat named Kofi Annan was chosen as the new secretary-general of the United Nations. I read an interview where he was asked how he had been so successful in bringing hostile factions together and to resolution at a negotiating table.

He told about a formative experience he had as a boy in an African school. The teacher had a large white chart up on the wall with a small black dot in the middle. He asked the boys what they saw on that wall. They eagerly said, "We see a little black dot."

He smiled and said, "That's strange. I see a big white chart with a tiny black dot on it." Kofi Annan explained that international conflicts often boiled down to parties fixated on a small black dot. His job was to get them to see that dot up against the much bigger white backdrop.

Our life here, with all of its hope robbers, is a small black dot. Compared to the panoramic sweep of the forever we're created for.

All the hope-draining dots of our life look and feel overwhelming down on the street. But when we can see them against the backdrop of eternity, they look very different. If there is sense, if there is hope to be found when we are breaking or broken, it will be with the view from the top floor.

That big-picture perspective on our hurting times has an unexpected effect. It starts us down a road of not only *feeling* our loss, but *asking questions* we might otherwise never consider. Those questions, explored in the next chapter, are bridges from hurt to hope. And the road to life-building, rather than life-damaging, choices.

We can think differently in our grieving because of the revolution made possible by the resurrection. Jesus added a transformative word to the word *life. Everlasting.* It's in the "everlasting" zone that we find meaning for our pain, healing for our brokenness, and hope for our "hopelessness."

It is our choices that determine whether life's hard hits take us to a bitter place or a better place. And the foundation for choices where hope wins is a cross on a hill and a tomb that is empty.

Standing there, we are ready to confront the hurt and the loss that make hope so hard to hang onto.

The Savior who carried a cross is there to help me carry my burden. And, when I am too weak to go on, He even carries me.

The unstoppable Man empowers me to bear the unbearable, face the unthinkable, and do the undoable.

This "Man of sorrows," having lived our grief and struggle, is closest when I am broken.

This Resurrection Man infuses me with renewing life when I feel like I'm dying inside.

This Savior who is weaving my life here into an eternal tapestry says in my dark time, "This isn't the story—this is only a chapter."

This death-crushing Jesus stands by me at a fresh grave and whispers, "This isn't the end. It's the *beginning*."

I echo the transcendent shout of Pope John Paul II: "Do not abandon yourselves to despair. We are the Easter people, and hallelujah is our song!"

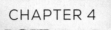

CHAPTER 4

THE QUESTIONS HOPE ASKS

When times are good, be happy; but when
times are bad, consider this: God has made
the one as well as the other.

ECCLESIASTES 7:14

You're living your baseball dream—playing in the World Series. Suddenly, the whole stadium starts shaking.

The San Francisco Giants were playing at home in the third game of that series. It was minutes before the game was scheduled to begin, and sportscaster Al Michaels was providing the pregame commentary.

I remember watching as the TV camera started shaking. A 6.9 earthquake rocked northern California.

Giants catcher Terry Kennedy immediately stopped warming up for the game and began to look for his family as fans fled the stadium. Later, a reporter asked him what he was thinking. His answer was insightful: "Sure does change your priorities, doesn't it?"

That's what happens when our world starts shaking. We start thinking. Asking questions we might otherwise never ask. Rethinking priorities we might otherwise never evaluate.

It happened to me in the most vivid terms the day my wife was suddenly Code Blue in the hospital. That was more than a decade ago. I almost lost her.

It was hard seeing her in cardiac intensive care, on a respirator, tubes everywhere. I kept telling her I loved her and giving her encouragement. It was all one way. She couldn't communicate at that point.

I knew she was coming back when her indomitable sense of humor prompted her to write the nurse a note: "The most exciting thing all day is when my blood pressure cuff inflates." Welcome back, my crazy lady!

In the hours when Karen's outcome was uncertain, I did some serious soul searching. And something happened in my soul.

I "retreasured" the woman I married. It wasn't that I'd ever stopped loving and valuing her. I had just let the relentless demands of my work sometimes leave her only my leftovers. Leftover time, leftover attention.

Code Blue for her was a wake-up call for me. Almost losing her rocked my world. When your life is shaken like that—well, "Sure does change your priorities, doesn't it?"

HAMMERS

Is a hammer constructive or destructive?

Yes.

It all depends on what you do with it. It can build a house or tear it down.

Are the life hammers that hit us hard constructive or destructive?

Yes.

It all depends on what you do with it.

When you lose someone or something you love…when the doctor has bad news…when there's no job, no money…when you've blown it big-time…when there seems to be no answer—you won't be the same as you were before. The hammer will change you, for better or worse.

But it's not the hammer that decides whether hurt or hope wins. We do. By the choices we make.

After a hit, I've seen people turn inward with self-pity or isolation. Turn hard with bitterness and negativity. Turn self-destructive, using damaging "pain relievers" to try to escape their pain. Or turn on the people around them, leaving loved ones scarred by a mean spirit and thoughtless words.

All too often, hurt people *hurt* people.

But I've also seen one of life's hammers build something beautiful in people. A tender heart for other hurting people. A recognition of an unwitting neglect of people they love—and a commitment to "retreasure" them. A realization and reordering of misplaced priorities. A repenting of a long-covered sin. A relationship with God that is more real, more passionate than ever before.

I've done it both ways. There have been times when the hammer made me hard. And other times when it made me softer, better.

And I've concluded that there are four hope-filled outcomes that can come from hurt-filled events: Revaluing. Recycling. Releasing. Rebuilding.

REVALUING—MISPLACED PRICE TAGS

Life has two lists. The things that really matter and the things that really don't. The lists get jumbled. Things that really matter drift over to the "don't matter" list. And things that really don't matter become way too important.

Then the storm hits.

You see it on the news when a family's home is destroyed by a fire or a tornado. Often, they will say, standing in the rubble, "My family's all okay. And that's all that matters." Or, "You can replace things. You can't replace people."

I guess the bottom line can be summarized pretty simply: *If you're going to get the pain, get the point!*

That's why the Bible's wise King Solomon said, "When things are bad, consider." And there are questions to ask that can lead us to some of the purpose in the pain.

> *What priorities do I need to reevaluate?*
>
> *What important things have I been neglecting?*
>
> *What regrets can I learn from here?*
>
> *What weakness or sin is this revealing in me?*
>
> *What have I done—or not done—that helped bring this on?*
>
> *What is God trying to say to me through this?*

Apparently, the Bible writer and Christian ambassador Paul had learned through his unrelenting trials how the hammers can build something beautiful. He wrote: "We know that suffering produces perseverance; perseverance, character; and character, hope. And hope does not put us to shame" (Romans 5:3-5).

Suffering → Character → Hope. Now that's a hope-filled outcome from hurt-filled events!

So, one question that hope prompts me to ask in my storm: *What really matters in my life—and what really doesn't?*

RECYCLING–TRASH TO TREASURE

"You just landed on the garbage of New York City."

That was the troubling newsflash my friend gave me when he picked me up at LaGuardia Airport. It didn't *look* like garbage. It looked like a runway.

But my friend pointed out to me that part of that airport was built on a landfill that extended out into the bay. And, of course, landfill equals lots of garbage. Recycled.

It's pretty amazing how engineers can take so many kinds of waste and trash and recycle them into something useful.

It's much more amazing how God can take the garbage of our life and recycle it into something useful.

I've been keeping a journal since my wife's homegoing. I want to remember the journey—and learn from it. In the weeks that followed, I wrote: "Lord, I don't want to waste this grief. If it's going to hurt this bad, please use it to make me more useful to You."

All I can say is that something's been happening in me that I find hard to describe. I know my heart is more tender toward others and toward God than I've experienced before. There's a new compassion.

And each day seems more important than ever. I have a refired sense of urgency about my life's mission. As Moses wrote, "Teach us to number our days, that we may gain a heart of wisdom" (Psalm 90:12). And Paul talked about "making the most of every opportunity" (Ephesians 5:16). I feel that in a new way.

I find myself thinking legacy more than ever too. I want to be more intentional about passing on to my children, to my grandchildren, to young leaders what God has taught me in my lifetime. As the Lakota proverb says, "We will be known forever by the tracks we leave behind."

I know the kind of tracks my wife left behind. They're recorded in the hundreds of notes and letters—*tributes*—I received about her after her homegoing. They had a recurring theme—"She made me feel… " Special. Loved. Important. Valuable. Like my life was worth living. Forgiven.

Those testimonies have sensitized me anew to how *I* make people feel when they're around me.

And there's something special going on between me and God. Maybe because a broken heart is an open heart. I had done my whole adult life with my baby. Suddenly, I was doing life without her—and there was no map.

It's as if God has taken me by the hand and He's leading me step-by-step through the dark as a father would do with his little boy. He just seems closer and His leading clearer.

Recently, at a convention, a ministry leader I respect pulled me aside and said, "I've been reading what you've been writing lately, Ron, and listening to what you're saying on your radio programs. And you are *speaking from a deeper well than ever before.*"

I doubt this book would ever have been written except for the greatest grief of my life. And the deeper well that has come from it.

I am experiencing the divine recycling miracle God says He will do in wounded people: "The LORD…has sent me to bind up the brokenhearted, to…provide for those who grieve…to bestow on them a crown of beauty instead of ashes" (Isaiah 61:1-3).

CRUD-ENTIALS

Beauty from ashes. That's the hope promise for those who are hurting. I'm seeing the ashes of my grief be recycled into the beauty of growth.

And that, in turn, seems to be spilling out into the lives of others. My heart has been opened up by being broken. I'm more transparent since I lost Karen. And as I speak or share, I'm finding that open hearts *open hearts*. My grief journey has given me a surprising platform from which to honor both my wife and, more importantly, her Savior.

When I say, "The Anchor holds," people really listen. Because of what I've been through.

It's a reminder of a hope-filled outcome that can come from hurt-filled events: crud-entials.

God recycles the worst things that have ever happened to us into credentials. Or *crud*-entials—that qualify us to speak of the difference Jesus makes in life's deepest valleys and darkest moments.

And people listen. People may not want to hear your message. But they will listen to your scars.

Each summer for the past 25 years, I have traveled with a team of heroic Native American young people. We've been to some of the most hope-starved places in North America—Native American reservations and First Nations reserves.

These young men and women have lived such pain and despair—the staggering suicide rates, the epidemic addictions, the sexual violence, the cycle of hopelessness—so much of which is rooted in the history of all that has been done to their people. But that's who they *were*. Today, they are bringing hope to thousands of their people.

They have found that hope where so many of us have found ours. In Jesus, Heaven's Rescuer. And when they tell their "hope stories" to crowds of pain-hardened Native young people, something supernatural happens. Their open hearts open the hearts of young people who desperately need that hope.

These young spiritual warriors are listened to as no pastor or missionary would ever be listened to. Because they come with *crud-entials*. It is the garbage of their life that opens hearts that have been closed for a long time.

When the worst happens, there is a question that erupts from our wounded heart: "Why, God?"

That question may never be answered this side of eternity. Eternity will answer all our whys. Until we can see the whole tapestry, many of the threads may not be understood.

But there is a question that *can* be answered here—a question that is the first step in finding meaning in our pain: "How can God use this?"

In January 2010, a catastrophic earthquake devastated Haiti, causing at least 100,000 fatalities. The answer to the question "Why?" may have as many answers as there were lives affected by the tragedy.

But one pastor's wife chose to ask the important question that *could* be answered. She said, "We survived. We can be sure that God spared us. The next question is, *Why?* What am I going to do with the fact that He spared my life? Will I be the same? Or how can I use it to care for others?"

Perhaps that perspective from the "top floor" suggests a more specific question: "How can God use this loss to give hope to others?"

That's when ashes become a crown of beauty. When hurt grows into hope. Defiant hope.

BEAUTIFUL BROKENNESS

There wasn't much left of the Japanese coastal city of Ishinomaki after the March 2011 tsunami. Just fields of debris where houses and tearooms once stood.

As Sue Takamoto was helping to clear away some of the debris one day, she noticed all the colorful shards of broken pottery that were everywhere she stepped. They were all that remained of tearooms and kitchens that had been swept out to sea.

Sue and her friends decided to collect and wash the shards. They saw in those broken pieces a way to help some broken lives. They began the Nozomi Project—Japanese for "hope."

The tsunami had left many single mothers without a job, without an income. So the Nozomi Project enables them to create rings and necklaces and earrings from rice bowl and teacup shards. The jewelry is then sold on the Nozomi website. Each woman names her line of jewelry, sometimes after a loved one who perished in the disaster.

Sue Takamoto summed up how ashes had been turned to beauty and devastating loss to triumphant hope:

> Many of these women lost their community—their neighbors are all gone. Their homes are washed away, and they're all living in scattered places across Ishinomaki. But God can take broken pottery and broken women who think that life is over for them and do anything He wants. We are in the midst of seeing God do amazing things. In the rubble of our storm, we all have lots of broken pieces. We can leave them broken. Or—with God's grace and help—make them into something beautiful. Something called hope.

CHAPTER 5

NOT MY BATTLE

I must accept finite disappointment.
But never lose Infinite Hope.

D**R**. M**ARTIN** L**UTHER** K**ING**

As the story goes, eagles welcome storms. While other birds run for cover, the eagle sits waiting for the storm's arrival.

Eagles soar on wind currents and updrafts. Something a storm has plenty of. So when that wind hits, it is said an eagle can use those currents to carry him higher and higher.

So can we. Our storms can ground us. Or they can carry us higher than we've flown before.

Again, it is our choices that determine the outcome. We don't get to decide if and when a life storm hits us. Or even what we lose in the storm. But we do decide where the storm takes us.

What we've lost can ultimately lift us higher as defiant hope chooses to pursue the hope-filled outcomes that can come from hurt-filled events.

In the last chapter, we explored two of those—and the hopeful question those responses ask:

- Revaluing

  What is God trying to say to me through this?

- Recycling

  How can God use this loss to give hope to others?

As we take God's elevator to the top floor to get the big picture of what's hit us, we can see two other hope-filled outcomes. If we make the right choices.

LET IT GO

I just happened to flip on cable news as they were showing a harrowing rescue incident. A young mother was trapped with her little baby on the second floor of a burning building. She was literally hanging out the window with her infant in her arms.

Down below, three men working nearby had heard her screams and came running. Now they were calling up to the young woman, assuring her they would catch her baby if she released him.

Initially, she shook her head—no way! But as the flames grew closer and the smoke thicker, she finally made the agonizing decision to let her baby go. All the men were waiting side by side, arms extended. The man in the middle caught the little guy!

Moments later, the firefighters arrived and ultimately rescued the mother. What struck me—and stuck with me—is how she later described the heartrending decision she needed to make: *I knew I'd have to let go of him if I was going to save him.*

That's a tough choice in many of life's painful moments. When your son or daughter is in open rebellion, hurtling toward some heart-breaking, even life-wrecking, choices. When you're desperate to try to save what's left of your marriage. When your business or your financial future is heading for the rocks.

When hope is slipping away, there's a choice to make. The intuitive response is to hold on tighter. To fight to hold on to control. Because we're afraid of losing something we need or cherish. But trying to hold it tighter often brings about the very loss we had feared.

There is another choice when hope is fading. It's counterintuitive. It's scary. But it is often the choice that is the hope of "saving the baby." Letting it go.

As we lose hope for a happy outcome, our tendency is to try to "make it happen." I want to be married, but I'm still single. So I push in relationships, often pushing people away. I get desperate. I manipulate. I compromise. I try too hard. I settle. Believing that some marriage is better than no marriage.

Only to discover that there's something lonelier than not being married. That's being married to the wrong person. Too many people I've met have found that to be the loneliest lonely of all.

But it's not just relationships where fading hope tightens our grip and yields a hurtful outcome. It often happens when financial disaster is looming. The bills are mounting. Our income may be shrinking. We're threatened with losing our credit…even our home.

Sadly, at that point, so many have, in desperation, tried to make things happen. Only to make things worse. Borrowing what there's no way to repay. Overheating credit cards, only to delay what will one day be a financial avalanche that buries us. Sometimes going to the extremes of gambling or even illegal activity to keep the ship afloat.

And the choice to control only leads to catastrophe.

Brian faced that with the family business. The business his grandfather had started. That his dad had expanded. Brian was able to enjoy the benefits as he lived his dream of being a race car driver.

Until one day, his father was suddenly gone, and the family business empire was his. With his father and grandfather gone, there was a sudden crisis of confidence among investors and customers—who began bailing out before Brian could even stabilize the company.

So Brian became a human machine that ran almost around the clock. He ate, drank, slept, and lived the business. He took on one court battle after another. He turned the business around, made it bigger than ever.

But it cost him his marriage. It cost him his health. Dealing with dark feelings he never could have imagined before, he sought professional help. The diagnosis stunned him: "Brian, you're suffering from dangerous clinical depression."

Brian told me, "I was a broken man."

And that's when, in the wreckage of hurt-filled outcomes, he made the hope-filled choice.

"I surrendered to Jesus. And gave everything to Him."

RELEASING

Over the years, both my wife and I have been marathon drivers. With me often insisting on the manly prerogative of being the lead driver.

As the hours on my driving binge got longer and longer, Karen learned the secret. When I started rubbing my right leg, we were about to die. Apparently, that was the first clue that I was starting to fade.

Karen would gently ask, "Honey, would you like me to drive?"

Why, of course not. "I'm fine."

Then came the loud music on some aggravating station.

"Honey, why don't you let me drive?"

That's crazy. No need. Now the window is down—and it's like 20 degrees outside.

Maddening music. Frostbite. Calisthenics behind the wheel.

"Let me drive, Ron."

Finally, I pull over. Just before we become a National Safety Council statistic. I'm out like a light before she can even get us back on the road.

As I've reflected on those times, I've wondered how many times God and I have played scenes just like that. I'm determined to drive. And He's asking, "Ron, why don't you let Me drive?"

But instead of relinquishing the wheel, I just tighten my grip on it. It's only a matter of time before I crash.

That's not just an imaginary scenario. I've done it. Like when I have wrestled with financial battles at work or when there have been interpersonal challenges with others. The control freak in me just wanted to hold on more. Praying, yes. Releasing, no.

I've never liked the outcomes.

I'm pretty sure I'm not alone in this battle for the wheel. Which seems to become more intense as the sky darkens and the ominous storm clouds make the sun of hope disappear.

My friend Kevin has pastored in a high-demand ministry for over 30 years. He may be the most looked-to man in his area when people are in need. Not long ago, he shared with me five words a spiritual brother had shared with him. They were actually spoken by John the Baptist, the wilderness preacher whose mission was to prepare the way for the coming of Jesus.

He told an adoring crowd one day, "I am not the Messiah."

Those are the five words. Liberating words for busy, make-it-happen people like my friend Kevin. For me.

Ultimately, I am not the fixer. The answer.

In fact, maybe sometimes God is trying to send us a life-changing message when there's a life-jarring loss.

"I'm God. You're not."

When that soaks in, you stop trying to control. And you start making the hope choice—releasing it completely to God.

It's what He's been waiting for, for a long time. But it's often not until a jarring loss or a crisis of hope that we finally raise the white flag of surrender. And we suddenly see that first glimmer of sunrise after driving through a long, dark night.

Because…

Relinquishing control allows God to do what only HE can do.

With a marriage. A business. A wandering child. A broken heart. A lonely heart. An "impossible" situation.

So, from a great loss can come a great question. One, that like the others mentioned before, can help us choose our way to a hope-filled outcome from a hurt-filled event. *What am I trying to control that I need to release?*

I was at a gospel concert one night, and I got ambushed. By a song. One line of that song vividly reminded me of the hope-awakening lesson I just need to keep relearning: *This is not my battle. This is not my war. I surrender.*

There's seldom a day that goes by now when I don't quote what has become a "North Star" Bible verse for me. A star to steer by, whatever that day, that journey, that situation may hold. "Commit your way to the LORD; trust also in Him, and *He* shall bring it to pass" (Psalm 37:5 NKJV, emphasis added).

These days, I don't wait until just before—or after—the crash to let Him drive. There's much more hope when I'm in the passenger seat and He's in the driver's seat.

On that fateful May day when I suddenly found myself in "the valley of the shadow of death," I was one lost little boy. Facing life without the love of my life, I had no map, no answers, no words for my feelings.

But I don't have to drive anymore. He knows where we're going. And, thank God, He's driving.

REBUILDING

Two massive hurricanes within days of each other. Harvey swamped Texas. Irma devastated Florida.

First, they talked about rescue—saving lives. Then came the long slog they call recovery. Weeks. Months. Years.

But the aftermath of Florida's previous monster hurricane, Hurricane Andrew, yielded some unforeseen good from the storm. Andrew's killer winds revealed fatal weaknesses in many buildings—and the need for much stronger building codes.

So, the rebuilding process did not just re-create the pre-Andrew landscape. It resulted in buildings constructed to withstand some of nature's most brutal winds.

As a result, Hurricane Irma, with all her punishing gusts, could not do what Andrew had done.

From the devastation of one storm came a new strength to withstand future storms.

That has happened in many a life, torn up by one of life's Category 5 storms. Heartbreaking losses. Life-altering medical hits. A shipwrecked relationship. Family crisis.

From the rubble of that storm came something stronger than ever before. And that is hope! Defiant hope!

We choose hope in the face of a great loss when we choose to revalue what's important…recycle our hurt into hope for other hurting people…release our control to allow God to do what only He can do… and rebuild around the hurt a more storm-proof us.

When we lose someone or something that has been a life anchor, it often leaves a gaping hole in our heart.

For me, that hole feels like the Grand Canyon. Karen and I were partners, buddies, confidants on so many levels. I miss her in a thousand ways.

A friend of mine who lost his wife to cancer five years ago has moved in alongside me as others did for him. He's checked on me, sent me resources that helped him, known the questions to ask, the prayers to pray.

He sent me an amazing quote from Dietrich Bonhoeffer that was a great light in my "valley of the shadow." Then he added his own observation that helped me set a course to hope.

Bonhoeffer, in *Letters and Papers from Prison,* starts with the bad news: "There is nothing that can replace the absence of someone dear to us, and one should not even attempt to do so. One must simply hold out and endure it."

I'm grateful for what follows:

> At first that sounds very hard, but at the same time it is a great comfort. For to the extent the emptiness truly remains unfilled, one remains connected to the other person through it. It is wrong to say that God fills the emptiness. God in no way fills it, but much more leaves it precisely unfilled and thus helps preserve—even in pain— the authentic relationship…one bears what was lovely in the past, not as a thorn, but as a precious gift deep within, a hidden treasure of which one can always be certain.

My personal summary: Karen being gone has left a gigantic hole in my heart. And that hole will always be there. And I want it to be. Because that's where Karen—and all the treasures of our life together—live in my heart.

Oh, how that helps me accept—even embrace—the void my grief has left.

My friend John—reflecting on his five years without Nancy—added the corollary lesson of his own journey: "You rebuild your life around that hole."

That's where I am now. Rebuilding after the hurricane of death seemed to level everything. I cannot live hopefully and make my loss what defines my life. I must not only rebuild *around* the hole in my heart—but *on* what I have learned from loss. That's a blueprint for hope.

So the final question that rises from the ashes of a great hurt is, *What have I learned from what I've lost that can make me stronger?*

My blueprint for a more storm-proof me includes so much of what I have gained from what I have lost.

- Treasure the people you love above any list, any schedule, any activity. While you can.

- Deal with what you regret while there's still time.

- Let your heart that broke keep your heart tender toward God and people. Don't ever let it close up.

- Take the elevator to the top floor to see the bigger picture God sees.

- Live each day as if you won't have another.

- Stay as real and raw with Jesus as you were at the point of your great loss. It allows Him to be closer than you've ever felt Him.

- Look for the people who need the comfort and caring that sustained you in your storm.

- The Anchor holds.

That's only a fraction of the lessons of a great loss. They are the building blocks of a life far deeper, far stronger than my life before the hurricane.

The hammer of a devastating loss can indeed build you or demolish you. But the hammer doesn't decide the outcome. We decide.

It is those *hope choices* that defy those *hope robbers* that come when we lose something or someone we treasure. In the chapters that follow, we will confront five storms that roar into our lives and threaten to sink us.

- Your broken heart—the grief from losing someone you love

- Your broken love—the wounds of a dying marriage

- Your broken dream—the discouragement and defeat of failure

- Your broken health—the fear and uncertainty when your future is in doubt

- Your broken past—the bitterness and bondage when the past poisons the present

When you check out the sports page to see team standings, their season will come down to *W*s and *L*s. Wins and losses. You won't find anyone with all *W*s. In sports. In life. Loss is going to happen. Some of those losses will be heart-wrenching, life-changing—and potentially hope-shattering.

You can lose a loved one. You can lose a job, a home, a dream. You can lose your health, your innocence, even an anchor relationship.

But you don't have to lose hope. If you make the choices that defy surrender.

On the dark horizon of trouble and tragedy is a sunrise that can light up the rest of your life. If you choose those hope-filled outcomes:

- Revaluing

    How can God use this loss to give hope to others?

- Recycling

    What is God trying to say to me through this?

- Releasing

    What am I trying to control that I need to release?

- Rebuilding

    What have I learned from what I've lost that can make me stronger?

A LOT OF DIRT AND A LITTLE GOLD

I saw it in a news report during a time of financial turmoil in America. The report came from Montana where they were furiously mining gold as it skyrocketed in value. Not gold nuggets. Just microscopic gold particles. One mine worker said, "You can't tell by looking at it that there's gold in it at all."

Actually, it looked like they were mining dirt. An armada of trucks was hauling dirt back and forth, night and day. The reporter said, "Getting the gold out is a massive task. They grind it, treat it, and heat it until they can finally squeeze out the good stuff. They move 190,000 tons of dirt a day—they'll get a few thousand ounces of gold."

What made the grueling process worth it was the end result—a 90 percent pure, 70-pound bar of gold. At that point, that gold brick was worth $1.25 million!

I can only hope that the extreme shaking and sifting and heat of my loss has produced something of value. To God. To those I love. To hurting people who will cross my path the rest of my life.

If I choose hope, gold can come from grief.

PART TWO

CHALLENGING LIFE'S HOPE ROBBERS

CHAPTER 6

HOPE WHEN YOUR HEART IS BROKEN

Grief is the price we pay for love.

ANNE LAMOTT

The blue chair. It is the daily reminder of the beloved woman we've lost.

My Karen had her share of health problems over the years, and that recliner served her well. Oh, she was "out and about" too, but when she was in our great room, that was her spot. And her headquarters. From which she touched hundreds of lives by phone, by text, by e-mail, by Facebook.

When her sudden, massive heart attack hit, that's where it happened.

One of the most heart-wrenching moments was our youngest grandchild's first time in that room after her homegoing. His four-year-old heart and mind just hadn't been able to comprehend his "Nali-Ma's" passing. Or even believe it. In fact, he kept insisting that his mom and dad were just joking with him. Until the day after when they brought him out to our house.

As usual, this human lightning bolt of a grandson ran full speed for the great room, his mother trying to keep up. By the time she got there, he'd been to the blue chair. He looked up and simply said, "You were right, Mommy. She's gone."

Those two words, spoken with childlike innocence, said it all for all of us.

She's gone.

We've been trying to figure out all that means since that day.

Oh, you can look up *grief* in the dictionary and find words that try to define it. Like "the emotional suffering one feels when something or someone the individual loves is taken away."

But there are no words to capture the anguish, the helplessness, the lonely cry of the human soul when you realize you've seen and held that cherished one for the last time this side of eternity.

You are gasping for the oxygen of hope. For us, with Jesus in the equation, we could quickly declare the resurrection-guaranteed hope of heaven's glory for Karen.

But we're not in heaven. Feeling like a knockout punch had just leveled me, I could not even begin to picture life without my lifetime love. Hope for Karen? I'm good with that part. Hope for us here—we were battling to find it.

Because grief may be the most powerful of all hope robbers. Many people never really come back from the knockout blow. They spend the next years lost…sometimes withdrawing to an emotional island all alone…maybe angry or bitter or just plain sad most of the time. Or making desperate choices to ease the pain—only to add to it.

In a blog entitled "The Best Grief Definition You Will Find," Russell Friedman offers a quote that fulfills what the title promises. Apparently, we don't know who said it—but they went far beyond a sterile dictionary description to the daily emotional reality: "The feeling of reaching out for someone who's always been there, only to discover when I need her (or him) one more time, she's no longer there."

That "reaching out" for my baby happens over and over again. Because she played a part in my life no one else could ever play.

I am strangely lonely. Strangely, because I'm blessed to be surrounded by family and friends who surround me with love. So many don't have that.

But Karen and I had—and I have lost—the one-of-a-kind love of a shared life. Where you've shared virtually every joy, every heartache, every battle, every relationship, every major life experience. There's no one else on this planet with whom I've lived my entire adult life.

So when I lost her, I lost our history. All the people—I just had to say a name. All the places—I just had to mention it. All the things we've laughed at—just say a word or a punch line. All the things we've prayed about…struggled with…cried over…celebrated and worried about in our kids. The list is endless.

But when I reached out to her about countless questions and decisions and fears, she had all the context of our lifetime. That all left when she left.

It's not like I'm crying all the time. My very busy life goes on. One day, searching for words to describe how all of us loved ones are feeling, I landed on a simple example.

I told my son, "It's like there's this upbeat, major-key tune playing constantly as the musical score of my life. But always—just underneath all that—is this quiet, minor-key score playing too. It's not usually dominant, but it's always there."

My son said, "That's it, Dad!"

Oh, every once in a while, it's like someone suddenly turned that underscore up full blast. It drowns out the brighter score that usually dominates. That's usually when the tears come.

"Mom-bushes" we call them. We got ambushed by an unexpected Mom moment or memory. They are sweet moments. Bittersweet.

Somehow, in the middle of the most broken moments of my life, I realized something that has ultimately spelled hope for me. Since I was hardly capable of thinking clearly, I can only assume that God led me to this game-changing conclusion: "I have to choose what I will do with this grief."

As lost as I felt, I did choose. I started a journal in an unused journal of Karen's. And days after she left, I wrote these words in bold at the top of the page: I WILL NOT WASTE THIS GRIEF!

MINING HOPE
FROM THE HURT

Back in the day, "going steady" couples sometimes wore a necklace in the shape of half a heart. And your "true love" (at least, at the time) had the other half of your heart.

While that may be just a little too much syrup, I get the idea behind it. Because on that dark day in May, it was like the other half of my heart was suddenly snatched away.

And I am convinced that no one who loses someone dearly loved can ever be the same again. The storm is too devastating. Too much of you left when they left. The hole is too big. The wound is too deep.

The question is, "What kind of person will you be because of your grief?"

That's where the choices come in. If you just go with the grief flow, chances are you will change for the worse. Angry. Bitter. Mean-spirited. Depressed. Paralyzed. Desperate. Withdrawn.

I realized I would have to choose what grief would make me if I wasn't going to waste the greatest hurt of my life.

The journal I began only days after my last day with Karen reveals a series of choices that, for me, have mined hope from the hurt.

Grieve Your Grief

I've known so many who haven't. They have stuffed their grief instead. Trying to appear strong. Not wanting to be weak or vulnerable. Quoting all the Christian "talking points" because Christians are supposed to be "okay"—whether they are or not.

Stuffed grief is like a beach ball pushed beneath the water. It isn't going to stay there. It's going to pop out somehow. And the farther down you push it, the higher it's going to go when it goes.

Because my wife and I have been so involved in the lives of Native American "sons and daughters" over the years, we've seen the destructive power of grief that is not truly grieved. In his book *The Grieving Indian*, Art Holmes (Ojibwe) identifies "unsettled grief" as a root cause of much of the addiction, anger, depression, and suicide that plague Native communities.

Over and over, in my work with people from all kinds of backgrounds, I've seen what a "monster in the closet" grief can be. Stuffed grief morphs into monsters. Including the anger, addiction, and depression I mentioned above.

Centuries ago, Shakespeare advised, "Give sorrow words." Then, he described the alternative: "The grief that does not speak knits up the o'er wrought heart and bids it break."

I gave sorrow words in my journal almost from day one. I wrote that "the sobs that came as we first entered Mom's great room with no Mom were awful. 'It hurts so much.' I just blurted it out."

Strange as it seems, I had to face the hurt to open the door to the hope. I remembered the comforting words from the Twenty-third Psalm: "He leads me beside quiet waters, he refreshes my soul" (verses

2-3). That's what I needed. My soul felt bullet-riddled and bleeding. If I was going to experience God's restoring, I needed to take some time by the "still waters."

It's not easy to get off the always-spinning carousel of my life, but I did. I wrote, "I must get away by myself to try to feel my feelings, hear God's voice, and get Jesus's perspective on this land without a map."

Pouring out the deepest wells of my grief to God—and opening my heart to His response—got my grief out in the open. While only God heard it all, I determined that I was going to be transparent with people about the pain of this loss. For if I was not real about the hurt, who would believe the hope?

As I write, it's a bright afternoon. But the stars are out. I can't see them, of course, but they're there. We just can't see their light except against the backdrop of a dark sky.

If I deny the dark sky of this season, no one will see how bright the stars of hope are.

I grieved my grief—and I continue to. If I don't deny my grief, I won't be defined by my grief.

It is as Jesus said: "Blessed are those who mourn, for they will be comforted" (Matthew 5:4).

Anyone who's ever lost a loved one knows how hard those "firsts" are. The first Thanksgiving without them. The first Christmas. And birthday. And vacation. And family milestones.

I think all of our family dreaded most the first anniversary of Karen's homegoing. Waking up that morning, again without my baby, I wasn't sure where my heart would land.

We can, for example, dwell on the final days or moments of our loved one's life. Focusing on how they died. What we wish we or someone else might have done differently. In a way, torturing ourselves.

Or we can dwell on the enormity of our loss. The longer Karen is gone, the more we experience the agony of her absence.

Celebrate More Than Mourn

I awoke on that dreaded anniversary to a text from a friend. It might as well have come from God. I'm convinced that's who inspired the message. "Praying that His JOY would overwhelm you."

That seemed unlikely. But he went on…

"His joy knowing your bride…is at this very moment worshiping in His throne room and looking into the face of Jesus. Ron, we love you and pray you celebrate more than mourn this day." "Celebrate more than mourn." That's where my heart landed that day. And many days since. That's the second hope choice I've made.

Rather than focusing on this side of eternity, I choose to focus on what my precious Karen must be experiencing on her side.

Like all of us here, she carried the wounds, the sadness, the burdens accumulated from living in a sin-spoiled world.

She carries them no more! All of life's sadnesses, gone in an instant!

The other day I told a nurse that I had just read about her being out of work someday. Then I shared the Bible's promise that "God will wipe away every tear from their eyes; there shall be no more death, nor sorrow, nor crying. There shall be no more pain" (Revelation 21:4 NKJV). Karen is living that!

And I think about the discovery conversations she is having with the spiritual giants of her history. And with those who walked with Jesus on this earth. And all those challenging questions her bright mind stumped me with—that she can now ask Jesus.

She's seen the nail prints in His hands. She's felt His touch. She's hearing His voice. She's touched the Glory.

And she's experiencing His pleasure for the life she lived so self-lessly for Him.

My baby's rugged journey here has ended. And I'm sad without her. But something healing has happened in my heart. I'm celebrating more than mourning.

Unpack the Regrets

Regrets. They're part of the sting of grief.

"I wish I had..." "I wish I hadn't..." "If only I..." There is often a heavy backpack we carry when grief surfaces the ways we failed—or think we failed—the one we love. And death allows no do-overs.

I have stood at Karen's grave and thought of so many things I wish I had done better or done differently. Two weeks after Karen went home, I wrote:

> Lord, never far away are my regrets for not loving Karen better. The times I disappointed her. That I spoke harshly. That she just waited to talk with me when I work, work, worked. If she walked in now, I would love her so much better. I will never have that chance.

I always told her that my favorite thing was to put a smile on her face. I know there were many times I did. It's those other times that add more weight to the grief.

There are still regret flashbacks—there probably always will be. But I have managed to confront those regrets and find a measure of release. By making a third hope choice to keep grief from defining me.

First, I had to dump the whole ugly backpack out at Jesus's feet. Some of that has come right at Karen's grave. God promised that if we "repent...and turn to God...[our] sins may be wiped out, that times of refreshing may come from the Lord" (Acts 3:19).

These sins were no different than others I've brought to Jesus. He died for every sin and shortcoming of my life. Including those that live in my memory as guilty regrets.

So, I am applying what Jesus did on the cross to all those things I should or should not have done to the woman I love. When, in His final moments, Jesus cried out, "It is finished!"—I know the word He used means "paid in full."

To the extent that I can learn to forgive what He has now forgiven, I can leave that backpack at His cross. Grief is heavy enough without the regrets.

It is also helping to really learn from those regrets. To do right what I did wrong before. So I don't have to remourn those regrets someday if I lose someone else close.

No one will ever know how much of my character and my work is because of Karen. She was God's mirror to encourage me to see what I could be and to challenge me to move beyond what I shouldn't be. She wasn't just my "better half." She made my half so much more than it would have ever been without her.

I can't go back and rewrite the past. But I can do what I wrote on the same page as I wrote about the regrets: "Please help me to be the man she challenged me to be."

Give Grace to the Grieving

Everyone's emotions are in the raw. Grief overwhelms the fences that usually keep our feelings in check. So with everyone so sensitive, it's really easy for people who love each other to hurt each other. Thus compounding the grief.

All too often, we expect everyone in the family to grieve as we do. We're crying—why aren't they? We're immobilized—why do they seem fully functional? We're talking about how we feel—why are they so quiet and uncommunicative?

It's easy to jump to the conclusion that if you don't grieve like I'm grieving, then you don't care like I do. Next come the accusing, hurting words. The last thing any of us mourners need.

Again, I wrote in my journal, "Each of us is expressing our grief differently, through the uniqueness of our personalities." One family member loved and grieved by doing, doing, doing in the days that followed our loss. Another was virtually overcome by deep soul sorrow—with frequent episodes of sobbing loudly and inconsolably.

Another family member was the one who kept extending grace and gratitude to those who were there for us—while being desperate to stop, pray, and work through the grief. Still another loved one just tried to deal with it privately on their own.

I expressed the hope choice I made in those raw-nerve days this way:

> I am learning that a massive loss is a time when we must
> give each person grace and space to grieve in their own way.
> Because no one can expect of another to be on the same
> timetable, expressing it the same way. But we also owe it to
> one another to gently and lovingly help make sure each of
> us gets our grieving and reckoning done.

In a word, I guess it comes down to respect. And not adding to a loved one's load our grief expectations.

Open Up to Jesus on That Lonesome Road

My wife grew up on a little Ozark farm—Laura Ingalls Wilder style. No electricity, no running water, and a bath with a path.

I was fascinated with what it took just for her to get to school each day. Mom saw little Karen off as she started the walk down the long dirt road to the bus. Next, Grandma watched from her porch until Karen was out of sight. Then, that kind neighbor lady.

And then the dark, lonely stretch to the highway. Her six-year-old imagination had plenty to imagine as she thought about the various critters that might be in those woods. She told me what calmed her fears. The song.

Every morning she would sing those comforting words: "Jesus loves me, this I know, for the Bible tells me so."

It was the daily dose of courage she needed.

Fast-forward to years later. Karen was on what would turn out to be her last conversation with her 94-year-old grandfather. "Hi, Granddad—this is Karen. I love you." After an awkward silence on the other end, Granddad replied, "I don't know who this is."

Karen reminded him that she was his only son's daughter—followed by "I love you." This time Granddad chuckled and said, "I'm sorry, but I don't know who this is."

Karen's response was inspired: "That's okay, Granddad. I just want you to know that Jesus loves you."

Granddad's response was unforgettable: "Now, Him I know!" He may have forgotten all the people who loved him—but one he couldn't forget. Jesus.

So a little six-year-old girl, at the beginning of life, walking that last dark stretch of road...a 94-year-old man, nearing the end of his life, walking that last stretch of life's road—both walking with the same "never leave you" Person.

The same Jesus who's been walking the loneliest stretch of road I've ever been on. And He's moved in closer than I've ever experienced Him before.

I decided to take Jesus up on a promise of His that I've shared with so many other grieving people. "The Lord is close to the brokenhearted and saves those who are crushed in spirit" (Psalm 34:18).

This final hope choice may have been the most helpful and healing of all...

I know there's another choice people make when someone they love is taken. They close up to Jesus.

Because they're hurt. They're questioning…struggling…even blaming God.

So they run from Him. When they need Him more than they've ever needed Him. He's our only hope of making any sense out of this loss. He's the only One with the spiritual resources to carry us through this dark valley. There is no "amazing grace" without Him. Only agonizing grief.

Oh, I'll have some questions for Him on the other side, for sure. What about Karen's unfinished work in so many lives—including our precious grandchildren? Why did I have to be gone that last day of her life? Why did her children have to have such vivid memories of her final moments?

But no questions could possibly be big enough to keep me from running to Jesus with my crushed heart. As Peter once asked when thousands of followers were abandoning Jesus: "Lord, to whom shall we go? You have the words of eternal life" (John 6:68).

So, yes, I opened up to Jesus. In fact, for me it went even one step further. Get desperate with Jesus! Get emotional with Jesus.

Maybe it's because I'm a guy, but I tend to have a more cognitive, left-brain relationship with Jesus. Sure, there are deep feelings, but I'm stronger on the factual side of knowing Jesus—Bible study, analysis, ideas.

But my heart was broken wide open. I didn't need answers. I needed to be held by Jesus. Carried by Jesus. I needed my Jesus to bring His comfort and love into the deepest corners of my shattered soul. And He did. He is.

The Bible recounts the miracle of Jesus walking on water as His disciples battled a life-threatening storm. At Jesus's invitation, Peter got out of the boat and miraculously began walking toward Jesus. Until "he saw the wind" and "was afraid." He began to sink. And prayed one of the shortest, most powerful prayers in the Bible. Three words: "Lord, save me!" (Matthew 14:30). And Jesus did.

When the grief tsunami engulfed me, that prayer was pretty much all I had in me. And, as He did for Peter, "immediately Jesus reached out his hand and caught" me.

I have learned that a broken heart is an open heart. Providing an opportunity for Jesus to go deeper into our heart than ever before. To plant a new sense of how loved we are and how strong His grace is. Beyond those wonderful verses—beyond those blessedly true Bible truths—is just this awesome Presence.

It may be what long-suffering Job was talking about when, after his series of unspeakable tragedies, he said to God, "My ears had heard of you but now my eyes have seen you" (Job 42:5).

My journal records my discovery in our house, when I was suddenly all alone: "Jesus is very big in this house today as I do my first day since the funeral parade ended. He is very big, very close, very real."

Three weeks into my life without my baby, I wrote, "It is You literally taking my hand as I would a lost little boy, and leading me moment by moment through my day."

He really is close to the brokenhearted.

Help Them Cry—Turn Your Hurt into Hope for Others

Little Wendy was never late walking home from school. Except this day. And Mom was suitably worried. Just before she was going to start making calls and drive around looking for her, Wendy walked in. To the predictable "Where were you?" questions.

"Mommy, I stayed extra with Amy—she was very sad because somebody took her dolly."

"Oh, then, were you helping her look for her dolly?"

"No," Wendy answered with soft eyes, "I stayed to help her cry."

There's a world of people out there who need someone to help them cry. I did. And my friend John helped me cry. He lost his wife to cancer five years ago. And though he travels a lot and we don't see each other much, he was there on the phone when he heard about Karen.

He knew what to ask. He knew what to say—and not say. He knew the resources that had sustained him in his deep loss. He knew what was ahead of me.

My friend was literally fulfilling a profound Scripture passage about finding meaning in our suffering:

> Praise be to the God and Father of our Lord Jesus Christ, the Father of compassion and the God of all comfort, who comforts us in all our troubles, so that we can comfort those in any trouble with the comfort we ourselves receive from God (2 Corinthians 1:3-4).

John had made a hope choice about his great loss. I made that choice too.

Four months after Karen's sudden homegoing, my friend Curt lost his wife suddenly. And I had the opportunity to walk some of his valley with him as John had with me. To comfort with the comfort I had received from God.

We can redeem our grief by deciding to use it to learn compassion. To open our heart, not only to God, but to a world of people who need someone to "help them cry."

If we close our heart, we will miss much of the meaning of our loss. For those who can make the greatest difference in this broken, bleeding world are the wounded healers.

I can honestly say that my heart is softer than it's ever been. I'm far less likely to be too busy for a wounded person than I was before. I'm far more likely to make that call, send that text, pay that visit when I hear of someone's loss or struggle.

The Bible describes Jesus as being "a man of sorrows and acquainted with grief" (Isaiah 53:3 NASB). Consequently, "we do not have a high priest who is unable to sympathize with our weaknesses," but one who is able to give us "grace to help us in our time of need" (Hebrews 4:15-16). He's walked our path—so we don't ever have to walk it alone.

My path of sorrows can be recycled into hope and compassion for others as they walk theirs.

My hope choice to find hope for others in my hurt became a prayer I prayed many times in my grief: "Jesus, if I must go through this pain, please use it to make me more useful to You than I've ever been before."

Defiant hope was born of a fundamental decision to not waste this grief. I knew I could never be the same after a loss this shattering. No one can.

If we don't choose, grief will make us harder rather than softer. More angry rather than more at peace. More about "me" instead of more about others. More alone instead of more connected. More closed rather than more open. More hurting instead of healing.

Hope is a choice. Not a feeling. Not a natural inclination. Not denial. A choice. It is a fist in the face of surrender.

HOPE, AFRICAN STYLE

Larry has dedicated decades of his life to translating the Bible into the Kisi dialect, spoken by many in Liberia. As often happens to Bible translators, he hit a word for which there was apparently no Kisi equivalent. And it's a word that's used in the Bible a lot.

Hope.

Repeatedly, he would try various words with his Kisi assistant, Tennyson. Every time, the reply was, "No, that's not it."

Larry was stuck. Until he needed to do some painting in his house. When he brought home several cans of paint, a man from the village eagerly asked, "Could I have the cans when you are finished with them?" Larry assured him the cans would be his.

Before sunrise the next morning, Larry was awakened by a knock at the door. It was that same man. "May I have the cans now?" he asked. Larry explained that he still needed to use what was in them.

The next morning—and the next morning—the eager villager was at the door again, checking to see if today was can day. Finally, Larry explained in detail how he had to use all the paint in the cans on the walls—then the cans would be his. At that point, the man responded in an unfamiliar phrase in Kisi.

When Larry asked his assistant what that phrase meant, Tennyson exclaimed, "That's it! That's our phrase for *hope*!"

Literally, the Kisi words mean "my eye is on the road for it." In other words, I'm not only looking at what's right in front of me, I'm looking for that better thing down the road.

That is indeed hope. Especially when you're standing there lost, with empty arms and a broken heart. That seems *hope*less.

Unless you lift your eyes. To what could come from this. The better, stronger, more caring you, forged in the fire of grief. And the glorious reunion that Jesus promised. Down the road.

My heart is heavy here. But my eyes are down the road.

CHAPTER 7

HOPE WHEN YOUR LOVE IS BROKEN

I will give you a new heart and
put a new spirit in you.

EZEKIEL 36:26

The man who officiated at Karen's and my wedding laughed at us on the way home. Oh, he didn't tell me that until years later—but he and his wife shared some amusing moments thanks to us.

As my minister friend and his wife were leaving the wedding, he said with a knowing smile, "They think they know so much about love, don't they?" Then they both just burst into laughter. Not because they were ridiculing us. But because they understood, as marriage veterans, how much we *didn't* know about love and marriage!

And they were right. I continued to learn what love and marriage mean our whole married life! As do most couples.

As I watched that beautiful brunette glide up the aisle in her white wedding dress, my heart was filled with hopes and dreams—and young love. I wasn't thinking much about the hard work of a happy marriage.

For most of us, love and marriage are where we place our highest hopes…our fondest dreams…our deepest emotional investment. And the place where, sadly, many experience the greatest hurt and disappointment of their lives. The one we love most can also hurt us most.

When romance turns to resentment and love creates more hurt than happiness, hope tends to head for the door. A marriage seems to be slowly dying. A breaking or broken marriage can crush hope as few other hurts in life.

And when a husband or wife loses hope, they start giving up. Thus, guaranteeing that they will continue to drift farther and farther apart.

Unless their hope is a *defiant* hope. The kind that raises a flag over the rubble and says, "I'm going to keep fighting for this love—wounds and all!"

Because defiant hope is "a fist in the face of surrender." As are the *choices* that keep hope alive.

LORD OF THE RING

The difficult but critical place to start is where it all began—the *vows*. Maybe that's one reason the man who married us was laughing. Because he knew how easy it was to promise—and how hard it could get to fulfill what was promised.

I don't know that I fully realized how serious those vows were until I read God's perspective on them in the Bible. I found it in the final book of the Old Testament where believers are frustrated that God doesn't seem to be hearing their prayers. He responds:

> You flood the LORD's altar with tears. You weep and wail because he no longer looks with favor on your offerings

or accepts them with pleasure from your hands. You ask, "Why?" It is because the LORD is the witness between you and the wife of your youth. You have been unfaithful to her, though she is your partner, the wife of your marriage covenant. Has not the one God made you? You belong to him in body and spirit (Malachi 2:13-15).

Apparently, that best man and maid of honor who signed our marriage certificate weren't the only witnesses at our wedding.

God was *the* witness to our vows. And He heard them as vows to Him. So much so, that failure to keep what He calls our "marriage covenant" comes between me and Him.

On our wedding day, Karen and I placed matching gold rings on each other's fingers. We were so committed to a lifetime love that we had these words inscribed on the inside: *Until Jesus Comes.*

Fast-forward to my recent shoulder replacement surgery. Since this was essentially my first real surgery ever, I was shocked when the doctor said my wedding ring had to come off. I hadn't had it off since my dear Karen put it on my hand those many years ago. I wasn't about to take it off now.

Until the doctor enumerated the risks of leaving it on. I finally agreed, knowing that they would have to cut it off because it wouldn't go over my knuckle.

When I awoke after the surgery, my adult children had the severed ring. With a piece cut out of it. But something amazing had happened. When I looked inside the ring, the words *Until Jesus Comes* were totally untouched! The jeweler who later repaired and resized it called it a miracle. Borrowing a phrase from J.R.R. Tolkien, I've come now to call God my "Lord of the ring."

Seeing those words intact was a pretty emotional moment. It was as if God was honoring our promised love—even with Karen and me on two different sides of eternity. He did hear our vows. And He never forgot them.

I believe He hears every couple's vows. So, as the classic vows echo from the Bible, "Therefore what God has joined together, let no one separate" (Mark 10:9).

Which is a powerfully compelling reason to choose hope over surrender in a struggling marriage. If God takes our promised love so seriously, then surely, we can expect divine help to heal what we cannot heal. To give us His strength to do what we are too wounded and depleted to do.

HEART TRANSPLANTS

The more we're hurt, the harder our heart tends to get. As disappointment and disillusionment increase, the conflicts escalate. The words escalate. And so do the wounds. As the Bible says, "The words of the reckless pierce like swords" (Proverbs 12:18).

Over time, the wounds from the one you have loved the most begin to erode that love. Hurt turns to resentment. And resentment starts to turn a heart hard.

And a hardening heart obstructs the lifeblood of a marriage—love. It was a tender heart that brought you together. It's a hard heart that will tear you apart.

And we can't fix our own heart. That takes a skilled surgeon. In this case, the One in whose heart marriage was born. The Master Heart Surgeon.

As I have prayed fervently for couples whose marriage was in trouble, I have staked my faith on a promise God has made: "I will give you a new heart and put a new spirit in you; I will remove from you your heart of stone and give you a heart of flesh" (Ezekiel 36:26).

The fundamental hope for any struggling marriage is a divine heart transplant. That turns a hardening heart soft again. That puts a "new spirit" in a man or woman to love again. To fight for this most sacred of all human relationships.

To make the hope choices that can help resurrect a dying love.

Those choices aren't easy—they're hard. They're costly. And they're risky. Because there is no guarantee how our husband or wife will respond. But they are choices that have the potential to bring about a new beginning. And that's worth the risk. Worth the cost.

Forget Winning

As battle lines emerge in a marriage, our pride starts insisting, "I must win. My spouse is wrong—and I'm going to show them." At some point, we stop listening. We've heard it all before. We aren't going to let them win.

When you insist on winning, you keep on wounding. And turn a heart even harder. We can't call it winning if, in winning a battle, we lose the war. If we lose the one we pledged our life to. Saving a marriage is about winning a heart, not winning an argument.

And the ancient wisdom of the Bible gives us a prescription for healing that goes against our fierce desire to be "right." It simply says, "Confess your sins to each other and pray for each other so that you may be healed" (James 5:16).

That statement suggests that healing begins with three words—three of the hardest words to get out of our mouth: *I was wrong.*

"I will if she will! If he will!" It can't work that way. Somebody has to risk being the vulnerable one. And no one can say they did everything they could to fight for their marriage until they are willing to confess where they have been wrong.

Maybe your partner is 90 percent to blame (highly doubtful). Then make your 10 percent right! We obsess on all the things our spouse has done wrong and quickly overlook or justify our failures.

But healing often begins with one person willing to admit being wrong. To forget *who* is right and focus on *what* is right. And even to ask for forgiveness for the wounds they have inflicted.

Expecting an immediate reciprocal response is unrealistic. It takes time for vulnerability to start to soften a heart with walls around it.

But an open heart opens hearts.

I read about a man whose eyesight had mysteriously deteriorated to the point where his vision was seriously clouded. It had been years when, making his way through a mall, he happened to walk into a pillar and sustain a hard hit on the head. But much to his amazement, he suddenly could see clearly! And later he said, "It's amazing! For the first time in fifteen years, I could really see my wife!"

Really *seeing* your wife or husband—that's key to hope for healing. And often it takes the "blow" of a marriage dying to help us see. Which reveals a second hope-giving choice:

See Your Spouse Through God's Eyes

That's not humanly possible. That kind of insight comes from God as you ask Him to help you see what He sees. The needs behind their deeds. The wounds behind their words. The poison from their past that affects them still today. The neglect they may feel. The place where all this unraveling may have started.

That kind of enhanced emotional vision helps a person get beyond reacting to the symptoms and into applying love to the real wounds.

Forget Fixing

You can remodel a home. You can't remodel a husband or wife.

But we sure try. There are sure to be cracks in a marriage when a woman sees her man as her project. To fix. But the more she pushes him to change, the less likely he is to change. As she talks louder, longer, and more often, he starts to shut down and stop listening.

And we men are instinctively fixers. As our wife unloads emotionally, our mind is already calculating how we can fix this. And her. Sadly, a man's approach to trying to change his wife becomes trying to control his wife. As she feels more trapped and smothered, she fights back. And slowly withdraws.

That's why there's so much wisdom in a well-traveled quote from Dr. Billy Graham's wife, Ruth. As a worldwide evangelist and "pastor to the presidents," he was gone more than he was home as his children were growing up. And yet all five of his children grew up to love and serve the Jesus he preached.

He and many others give much of the credit to the strong woman he married. All who knew her testified to her unshakable faith, her unvarnished honesty, her practical wisdom, and her inner strength. Billy Graham said, "My work through the years would have been impossible without her encouragement and support."

But for all her strength, Ruth Graham had a clear view of what she believed her job was. And wasn't. She said, "My job is to love and respect Billy. It's God's job to make him good."

There's a word for that—a hope word we visited in an earlier chapter. *Release.*

Our efforts to remodel our spouse are met not with change, but resentment. And resistance. And two hearts turning harder—because your spouse is trying to "fix" you. And because your spouse refuses to be fixed.

If indeed it's God's job to change people, then our efforts to do His job actually hinder what He's trying to do.

Our best hope for changing our spouse is to stop trying to change our spouse. And to say, "God, he (or she) is all Yours. Help me to help him (or her) feel safe and loved enough to take the risk of changing."

That release lets God do what we could never do—give our spouse "a new heart" and a "new spirit." Removing a "heart of stone" and replacing it with a soft "heart of flesh" (Ezekiel 36:26).

Download Bigger Love

The angry words, the cold rebuffs, the painful insensitivity—they can take a serious toll on even a strong love. But to resurrect a marriage, love is not optional. But what if feelings of love have been seriously eroded by all the hurt? That's when a cry for help to heaven is the sound of hope:

> God, I know You love him/her—but I'm just not feeling love at this point. I don't have a lot of love to give right now. But I'm willing to have You love my spouse *through* me. If You put Your love for him/her in my heart, I'll be the channel to deliver it. I need *Your* love for the person I married.

The most powerful form of prayer is praying based on something God has promised. And you can pray for a download of His love based on a promise like: "It is God who works in you to will and to act in order to fulfill His good purpose" (Philippians 2:13). Both the "want to" and the "how to" come from God, not from you.

Get Outside Guidance

Marriages often die of pride. Because both a husband and wife are unwilling to simply admit, "I need help." And "before a downfall the heart is haughty" (Proverbs 18:12).

There are people who have walked this trail with many other couples. A trained counselor can see things we can't see in the middle of our pain. And say things we might not listen to from anyone close to us.

Seeking outside counsel is not a sign of weakness, but a sign of strength. It's the sign of a fighter who is not willing to give up on a marriage. It's a sign of biblical wisdom because it demonstrates "the humility that comes from wisdom" (James 3:13).

A seriously ill person should not die simply because they would not see a doctor. A marriage should not die because a man or woman would not see a counselor.

If you cannot agree to go as a couple, at least seek counsel yourself. That third party perspective will at least give you a better understanding of you and your spouse. And what steps you might take to promote healing. "Instruct the wise and they will be wiser still" (Proverbs 9:9).

FOUR REDEMPTIVE QUESTIONS

I was speaking to a group of businessmen about how seriously God takes our wedding vows. And I told them the awful feeling I know all too well when suddenly there are no more days to love and cherish your wife. I suggested four questions that could head off what could be some painful future regrets:

- What would my wife say is her biggest competition for my time and attention?

    Sports? The Internet? Video games? My job? My hobby? My work at church? The best way to make your wife (or husband, for that matter) feel loved may be to consciously and consistently put them ahead of their biggest "competitor."

- In what specific ways have I become a better man because of her love and influence?

    Tell her. While she's still here to hear it.

- What are some qualities you love and appreciate about her?

  *Often, we're more in touch with what we don't love
  and appreciate about our spouse. It's time to turn
  the lens on some of the qualities that made you love
  her in the first place.*

- If she was suddenly gone today, what would my regrets be?

  *Clearly, the time to face that is while there's still
  time to fix it.*

THE CROSSROADS OF DIVORCE

My friend Jim is a brilliant engineer. Who may be a bit photographically challenged.

He and his wife were vacationing in the charming beauty of Cape Cod. Jim wanted to capture a shot of that beauty in a cell phone "selfie." With him against the backdrop of the majestic Atlantic Ocean.

Later, as he was reviewing his photos from the day, he lamented to his wife, "I missed the ocean."

"What?" she asked.

"Yeah…somehow all I got in the picture was me."

No offense to my highly intelligent friend, but how do you miss something as big as the ocean? Answer: by having the picture be all about yourself.

Which is what can happen when a breaking marriage becomes officially broken. Divorce. One of life's most heart-wrenching, life-upending experiences. And one that propels a person into an emotional danger zone where bad choices can just compound the trauma, not only for the husband or wife, but for others affected by the tremors from this quake.

And generally, the road to more wounds after the divorce is like my friend's disappointing ocean selfie. A picture that turns out being "all about me." And missing the hope factors within our reach.

It's a mistake that's all too easy to make when you've gone through the brutal hope robber of divorce. What was once your dream became a nightmare. What was supposed to be your safe place has become your battlefield. On the Holmes-Rahe Stress Inventory, which ranks life's major stresses in terms of the likelihood of them causing health issues, divorce comes in number two. Only the death of a spouse or child is potentially more destructive.

Your emotions are all over the place. Relief. Often mixed with regret. A sense of freedom. But also a sense of failure. What was once love is now a tangle of anger, loneliness, sorrow, bitterness, anxiety about the future.

So you're thinking survival. Emotional survival. Financial survival. Relational survival. It's hard to think about anyone else when I'm just trying to make it through this. It's survival mode—and survival is inherently about "me." "Nobody else is going to look out for me. I have to look out for myself now."

Understandable. But dangerous. Because, like all of life's major hits, the loss brings us to a crossroads. Where we again stand facing the road to hope and the road to more hurt. And more hurt is the last thing we need when we've gone through one of life's most painful experiences.

Ultimately, it won't be the divorce or our "ex" that determines which road we're on. It will be our choices.

I've seen how those choices play out in many families I've known and worked with over the years. Some that compounded the hurt. Others that led to healing.

No two broken marriages are the same. No two divorces are the same. But the choices that follow a divorce are usually similar, no matter what the individual circumstances. The ones that lead to healing are often counterintuitive amid the swirling emotions of the end of a marriage. But they are the choices that contain the damage rather than compound it. The choices of a defiant hope.

They begin with a courageous confrontation with the powerful emotional offspring of any death—including the death of a marriage: *grief.*

Take Time to Grieve

Many describe divorce as being a kind of death. And it is. The death of hopes and dreams, love and security.

As I've written earlier, when you've lost someone you love as I have, healing starts with grieving. It's true of divorce too. Not blaming or withdrawing or denying—but allowing yourself to feel the feelings of what you've lost. That's one reason I decided to start a grief journal where I could open my heart and let the feelings flow.

Journaling your grief journey can often help you process what you otherwise might try to bury or postpone. But for it to be a bridge to healing, it should chronicle your hurt and regrets and struggles rather than indicting your "ex" and enshrining bitterness in print. It's a grief journal, not a grievance journal.

For me, it's been healing to make God my audience for the grieving I'm putting into writing. He "gets" me like no one else ever could. I'm safe with Him and secure in His love. So there's no holding back. I am accepting the counsel of Scripture to "trust in Him at all times…pour out your hearts to him, for God is our refuge" (Psalm 62:8).

There's value, too, in facing your raw feelings with a counselor, a pastor, or a wise and trusted friend. Writing your journey, verbalizing your grief are important steps on the road to healing. Because what you don't deal with now, you will deal with later—after it's morphed into something much more destructive.

So the crossroads choice after a divorce is, *Shall I grieve my grief or stuff my grief?* The first road leads to healing. The other to compounded sorrow.

Don't Let Your Wounds Get Infected

My wife kept this little chart handy in our bathroom. It was a list of common poisons that a family member might ingest—and the remedies to use in an emergency.

Bitterness does not appear on that list. But if there was a similar list of emotional poisons, bitterness might be at the top, along with hate and resentment and anger.

The Bible surely outs bitterness as a troublemaker: "See to it that no one falls short of the grace of God and that no bitter root grows up to cause trouble and defile many" (Hebrews 12:15).

Bitterness is like a growing cancer. If it is not stopped early, it metastasizes, reaching far beyond the place it started.

My heart aches as I think of the young people (and even adults) I've counseled whose lives have been damaged by bitter seed sown by a divorced parent. Who, in trying to get their child "on their side" or to punish their "ex," tore down the other parent again and again. In the Bible's words, "defiling" others with the darkness in our own heart.

When God included "honor your father and mother" in His Ten Commandments, He didn't put an expiration date on it. And we undermine His clear imperative when we give a son or daughter reason to *dishonor* either parent. When we influence a child to, in essence, divorce their father or mother, we are defying a serious divine directive.

And bitterness is like a toxic waste dump—it leaks poison. The "root" of bitterness cannot be contained to one relationship with a person who wounded us. It "causes trouble and defiles many." So any emotional toxins we sow in our children are likely to one day poison their own family and close relationships.

There is no doubt that the wounds from a collapsing marriage go very deep and last very long. Because the people we love the most are also those who can hurt us the most. The wounds are real and painful. But there is one thing worse than a deep wound. And that's a wound that gets infected.

When we harbor dark feelings, however justifiable, we allow the wounds they inflicted to become dangerously infected.

That's why the hardest choice is the healing choice—choosing to forgive. There is much more about forgiving in a subsequent chapter, "Hope When Your Past Is Broken." But as hard as forgiving is, unforgiveness hardens your heart, infects other relationships, and gives the one who hurt you permission to live rent-free in your heart.

So a second "hurt or hope" choice after a divorce asks, "*Will I let my bitterness grow or will I let it go?*"

If there were a list of emotional poisons, headed by bitterness, the prescribed antidote would indeed be forgiveness.

Forgiveness paves the way for a third choice that invites hope into what's broken.

Try to Leave Some Bridges

Burned bridges can extend the hurt of a divorce and further complicate an already challenging future. Clearly, there are some situations where there are mitigating issues related to abuse, financial or legal conflict, or even physical danger that may make maintaining contact unwise. But with the exception of those extremes, maintaining some bridges of communication and cooperation is a vote for hope rather than more hurt.

There is wisdom in the counsel of Scripture that tells us: "If it is possible, as far as it depends on you, live at peace with everyone" (Romans

12:18). And Jesus said, "Blessed are the peacemakers, for they will be called children of God" (Matthew 5:9).

The lives of children still living at home as a marriage unravels and ultimately dies carry divorce scars as well as their parents. When walls rather than bridges are built between the divorced mom and dad, life for their children gets even more complicated. Because they have to negotiate on their own two of everything—two Thanksgivings, two Christmases, two birthday parties, etc.

When divorced parents commit themselves to doing all they can to minimize the "collateral damage" to their kids, they are choosing hope for both their children and for themselves.

So a third choice that can pave the way to healing—if we choose rightly—is, *Will I build walls or bridges in my relationship with my "ex"?* The sign on the bridge says, "This way to hope."

I'm pretty sure it's posted in every sports locker room in America. And it must be in that manual of motivational sayings I'm pretty sure coaches have hidden in their drawer: "No pain, no gain."

The issue after a divorce is, *Will it just be pain, or gain from the pain?* That depends in large part on making the next healing choice.

Learn from the Loss

It's true of all of life's "hammers." There are lessons to be learned and growth to be nurtured if we're willing. After my wife's homegoing, an entry in my grief journal suggested that I was hoping for gain from the greatest heartache of my life: "God, help me not waste this grief. Please use it to make me more useful to You and others." The earlier chapter on grief describes how God's been answering that prayer big-time!

Reflection on a painful experience—especially when it involves some personal soul-searching—is not easy. But it can help redeem some of the brokenness. Maybe that's one reason Scripture says, "When times are good, be happy; but when times are bad, consider" (Ecclesiastes 7:14).

There's not much to be gained from analyzing the mistakes your "ex" made that contributed to the unraveling of your relationship. There is much to be gained from reflecting on your own mistakes. What have I learned about how I communicate—or don't communicate? About how I show—or don't show—love and respect and appreciation? About any hurtful ways I handle conflict? About storing up wounds and disappointments and resentment? About my willingness—or unwillingness—to admit wrong?

I am always very adept at listing what's wrong with the other person—and pretty resistant to looking in the mirror to see my failures. But that's where growth comes from.

And that's where the gain from the pain comes from.

So, another after-divorce crossroads question: *"Shall I focus on what my 'ex' did wrong in our relationship or on what I could have done better?"* The one road traps me in the past. The other one prepares me for a more hopeful future.

Vulnerable. The dictionary says it means "capable of being physically or emotionally wounded."

Like after a divorce. It's true of many of life's great losses. Because of your pain, it's easy to make some decisions you will later regret. Jumping into another relationship. Living irresponsibly. One-night stands. Gravitating to friends who will drag you down. Self-harming or self-destructive actions. Feeding your mind with dark or dirty input. Seeking revenge. Neglecting your kids. Focusing on yourself. Experimenting.

When the wounds are fresh, they tend to distort your judgment. When your emotions are roller-coastering, they can lead you to what looks like a stream, but it's only a mirage. When you're lonely, you can grab at "love" and end up used and compromised.

That's why the next hope choice is so vital.

Secure Your Reservoir

Since you are vulnerable, you shouldn't make any important life choices until you've had time to stabilize and heal.

It's wise to fortify yourself with some friends who know you well, whose lives are in order, and who aren't afraid to hold up a mirror for you. Because "two are better than one...if either of them falls down, one can help the other up...though one may be overpowered, two can defend themselves" (Ecclesiastes 4:9-12). Accountability is an important step to protect your future while the wounds from your past are fresh.

And it's important to protect your reservoir.

I've read security specialists warning that one possible target for a terror attack might be some of our nation's reservoirs. That makes sense. They could poison the drinking water of thousands just by polluting the source.

Our emotional and volitional "reservoir" is our heart. And God warns us to be in the "homeland security" mindset when it comes to our heart: "Above all else, guard your heart, for everything you do flows from it" (Proverbs 4:23). Secure your reservoir!

That's exponentially important after losing a major life anchor. Like your marriage. So guard what music you listen to. The friends you hang out with. The things you read and watch. The websites you visit. The social media connections you make.

These are all tributaries flowing into the source of our life choices—our heart. It needs to be guarded. Fiercely guarded. Because our wounds make us vulnerable. To choices that will make the hurt of divorce into even greater hurt that's self-inflicted.

So once again, a great loss leaves us with choices between what will hurt us and what will heal us. Another crossroads choice: *Will I indulge myself because I'm hurting or protect my future with "no regrets" choices that will keep me safe?* The last thing a wounded soldier needs is more wounds.

I was in Rome for 18 hours between flights. Time to sleep? Not a chance! Not when I had time to actually see some of the sights of that fascinating city.

Thanks to Dave, a friend in Rome, I got to see a lot! Beginning with the history-echoing Colosseum. As we left, we were suddenly surrounded by a swarm of street children, grabbing at us from all directions. My friend had warned me of the possibility of just such an effort to try to grab something of value from us.

Dave managed to disperse them with the help of the umbrella he was carrying on our misty day in Rome. I had left most of my valuables in a locker at the airport. I checked to make sure my wallet and camera bag were okay. All secure.

We had walked a couple of blocks when a little girl came running over the hill, waving something blue in her hand. It was my passport! I don't know how they managed to get it out of the vest pocket in my sport coat, but there it was. I couldn't believe it. Thankfully, God looks out for me much better than I look out for myself sometimes.

I began to think about the implications for my onward trip to speak in Africa if I had lost my passport. After all, it's my identity! And it had been stolen.

Of course, in our online world, we know there are thieves trying to steal our identity all the time.

But in our personal world, there are other ways we can lose our identity. Through the lies we believe about ourselves because of how we've been treated. Or how we've suffered.

And the trauma of divorce can brand you with an identity that isn't you—if you let it. Which leads us to one more choice at the crossroads of hurt and hope:

Define Yourself by Your Unlosable, God-given Identity

You may have to fill out some forms that ask for your marital status, and you'll have to reply "divorced." But that's not who you are.

Since people tend to lump us together in categories rather than get to know us as individuals, there may be some who categorize you as "divorced." But that's not who you are.

You even look in the mirror sometimes and see "divorced." But once again, that's not who you are.

You are who God says you are. And we are not what we do. Or what we have done. Or what people may call us. Or how people treat us.

You are a person made in the image of the God who created you. You are a one-of-a-kind "God's workmanship" (Ephesians 2:10 NKJV). You were "knit...together in [your] mother's womb...fearfully and wonderfully made" (Psalm 139:13-14). You are created with a unique Creator's design for your life: "'I know the plans I have for you,' declares the LORD, 'plans...to give you hope and a future'" (Jeremiah 29:11).

Most telling of all, the Scriptures reveal how much you are worth to God. It says of Jesus that He "loved me and gave himself for me" (Galatians 2:20). That horrific death Jesus died on a Roman cross was actually Him sacrificing His life on your behalf. So every wrong thing you've ever done could be forgiven and you could be with Him forever in heaven.

No desertion, no abuse, no accusation, no injustice, no divorce can steal your God-given identity. Your God-given value.

So the final "hope or hurt" choice is, *Will I define myself by my divorce or by my unlosable, God-given identity?* There's so much more hurt with one. And so very much hope with the other.

Of all the many people I know who have run the gauntlet of divorce, there is a common characteristic in those who have emerged healed, restored, and hopeful.

The Jesus factor. They have wrapped their hope around the divine promise that "if anyone is in Christ, the new creation has come; the old has gone, the new is here!" (2 Corinthians 5:17).

They know their failures have been forgiven; their wounded heart is being restored; their future is in God's good hands; they have a love they will never lose.

That is hope.

HOPE FOR HUMPTY DUMPTY

The story of the not-so-smart egg was planted in my brain when it was young and fertile. Humpty Dumpty. The egg who came out of his shell and went to pieces. According to the classic nursery rhyme:

> Humpty Dumpty sat on a wall,
> Humpty Dumpty had a great fall;
> All the king's horses and all the king's men
> Couldn't put Humpty together again.

If you're in a Humpty Dumpty marriage—or the damage left in the wake of a marriage that's over—you can easily feel that there are too many broken pieces for anyone to put together again. But I have learned that, in human relationships, we should add one more line to this rhyme about brokenness:

All the king's horses and all the king's men
Couldn't put Humpty together again
But the KING CAN!

I know that King Jesus can do what no one else could do—put the most broken marriages, the most broken people, together again. I've seen it. Many times. Hope for a breaking marriage or a broken person has a name. His name is Jesus.

The battle to save a painful marriage is a battle worth fighting. And a battle no one has to fight alone. Not if a struggling wife, a struggling husband—better yet, a struggling *couple*—declares from the depths of their soul, "The battle is the LORD's!" (1 Samuel 17:47). And cries out the desperate, three-word prayer of Peter as he was sinking in the storm: "Lord, save me!" (Matthew 14:30). Better yet, "Lord, save *us!*"

The Bible records where Jesus did His first miracle: "A wedding took place at Cana in Galilee" (John 2:1). It was a miracle of transformation—water into wine.

Jesus still does marriage miracles. Miracles of transformation. That's why hope is still alive.

Defiant hope!

CHAPTER 8

HOPE WHEN YOUR DREAM IS BROKEN

Though I fall, I will rise again.

Micah 7:8

We're introduced to failure early. When we're a baby learning to walk.

I've watched a lot of kids take their first steps. And the script is almost always the same. They pull themselves up, holding on to a piece of furniture. Then comes that daring moment when they let go and try walking on those wobbly spaghetti legs.

Then...step. Boom!

Their dream of getting around independently like those big folks now lies "splat!" on the living room floor. What to do?

A little internal voice says, "See, this is too hard. You tried and you failed. Might as well forget walking." Fast-forward 18 years, and there he is, still lying on the living room floor with his mother vacuuming around him.

But babies don't do that. They get back up—and go step, step, boom! Then step, step, step, step, boom. Until eventually, it's all steps and no boom. And that kid is off and running for the rest of his life!

It's not as easy to get up and go again with the big hits that big people experience. Especially when it's a cherished dream that falls apart.

When something or someone we had placed our hopes in fails us. Or we fail ourselves.

And suddenly, hope is on the ropes. We are facedown in the ring, and the count has begun. Are we down for the count? Or will we get back in the fight for another round?

The cold reality is that it's hard to hang on to hope when your dream is in shambles. When the business you poured so much into dies. Or the workplace you gave your best to suddenly "doesn't need you anymore." Or you realize that the goal that's driven you for so long just isn't going to happen. The retirement you've dreamed and planned for is shattered by health or financial disaster.

But it's relationships that mean the most. And where a sense of failure hurts the most. A failed marriage. The feeling that you've failed as a parent. The dream of being married looking like it's never going to happen. The hope of having children of your own that now seems impossible.

And then there are the spiritual disappointments. The spiritual crash that seems to have left you feeling so far from a God who once was so close. Or the ministry dream that has now turned to disillusionment.

Failure has many faces. But one, all-too-common effect: the temptation to give up. To succumb to the powerful pull of despair. Of despondency. Of resignation and retreat.

When failure—whether you're to blame or not—leaves you with two choices. One, resign yourself to staying in this valley. Or, resolve to build on its lessons.

As always, hope must be a choice. A courageous, often counter-intuitive choice. Defiant hope. That doesn't let failure be final.

REBOUND

When you've been knocked down—or even knocked out—it's good to listen to some advice from a noted contemporary philosopher: Rocky Balboa. Who, from his legendary boxing career, knows plenty about knockdowns and knockouts. In the movie, *Rocky Balboa*, he tells an aspiring young boxer:

> The world ain't all sunshine and rainbows. It is a very mean and nasty place, and it will beat you to your knees and keep you there permanently if you let it. You, me, or nobody is gonna hit as hard as life. But it ain't how hard you hit. It's about how hard you can get hit and keep moving forward.

You have to choose your way to going another round. With the choices that restore hope after a knockout.

Choose to Resist the Lie That Failure Makes You Worth Less

"I failed." "I'm a failure." The difference between those two conclusions is all the difference between choosing hope and choosing surrender.

Failing may be what happened. But "failure" is never who you are. Because you were given intrinsic value by your Creator before you were ever born.

The Bible describes you as being "fearfully and wonderfully made"—from the time God "knit" you together in your mother's womb (Psalm 139:13-14).

You are what I told each of our grandchildren right after they were born. You are "God's workmanship, created in Christ Jesus to do good works, which God prepared in advance" for you to do (Ephesians 2:10). So no one on earth gave you your worth. And no one on earth can take it away. No financial failure, no family failure, not even any spiritual failure can diminish your worth.

So success doesn't mean you're worth more. And failure doesn't mean you're worth less. But if you believe the lie that you are worth less, you will start down the self-destructive road of "Oh, what's the use?" choices. You'll never rebound if you believe that when you lost your dream you lost your worth.

As Rocky says, "Our greatest glory is not in not falling, but in rising every time we fall." Better yet, as the Bible says, "Though the righteous fall seven times, they rise again" (Proverbs 24:16).

Allow God to Show You the Lessons in Losing

Generally, we don't go see a doctor just because we'd like to visit. Usually, some kind of pain, some physical dysfunction compels us to see him.

Sometimes that means tests. X-ray. Blood test. CAT scan. Sometimes they expose something that might not have been seen otherwise. And that may be the first step to going from sick to well.

The pain of a broken dream can have the same effect as those medical tests. It can expose something that might not have been revealed otherwise. Something that needs to be removed or repaired.

So there's a second hope choice that makes rebound possible rather than resignation: Allow God to reveal how He wants you to grow through this.

I know what some of my failures in leadership have made me face. Over the years, my failure to confront has caused me to let relatively minor problems or conflicts become monstrous problems or conflicts.

Fires can be contained when they're small. Ignore them, and they will destroy more than you could have imagined.

Through the pain of letting fires get too big to contain, God showed me something about myself I didn't want to see. My fear of what people would think of me. My desire to please subverting my strength to lead. I didn't confront because I feared losing their favor or respect. The resulting fire cost me that and more.

My leadership failure could have driven me into retreat. Or to reevaluate, repent, and rebound. As a more courageous leader.

Hope won because I finally allowed God to show me where I needed to grow. But it took pain to get me to "the doctor."

THREE FATAL FLAWS

Often, the lessons of losing reveal three areas critical to our growth, our future success, and the future blessing of God. Three fatal flaws that we might never see and deal with except for the pain of failure.

Our Pride

Let's face it. Sometimes it takes failing to show us how much ego there was in succeeding. Often, pride has to be wounded to be cured. And God treats pride like the spiritual cancer it is. As Bible scholar William Barclay said about pride, "It is the garden in which all other sins grow."

According to the Bible, pride was so powerful that it cost Lucifer, the most beautiful of the angels, heaven. As his beauty and gifts made him decide, "I will make myself like the Most High" (Isaiah 14:14), he was cast out of heaven. And became Satan, mortal enemy of every human soul.

Pride was so powerful that it cost Adam and Eve paradise. As Satan used the same lie on them that cost him heaven: "You will be like God" (Genesis 3:5).

Pride destroys. So, in His love, God uses our losses as divine pride busters. Because He knows the hidden motive for many of our personal dreams: pride. "All a person's ways seem pure to them, but motives are weighed by the LORD" (Proverbs 16:2).

Pride has many faces. Parent pride. Position pride. Professional pride. Academic pride. Beauty pride. Fitness pride. Leader pride. The pride of being "looked to," of having our own way, of having the answers.

The divine Heart Surgeon wants to replace the stench of pride with the fragrance of humility. "'God resists the proud, but gives grace to the humble.' Therefore humble yourselves under the mighty hand of God, that He may exalt you in due time" (1 Peter 5:5-6 NKJV).

It's possible that one reason for a broken dream is God "resisting" the pride behind it. And pride hides—it's too proud to admit what it is. But I have experienced those times when failing is what exposed how much "me" and "my way" there was in my dream.

Which opened the door to seeing me as God saw me. And the pain over my loss drove me to my knees. And to the humbling that brought me healing. And sometimes, even healing to my situation. Because God could now trust me with success.

When you bring the broken pieces of your dream to Jesus, you may find treasure there. Less of you, more of Him. The humility that God loves to bless and honor.

The shock and sadness of failure can be God's X-ray to reveal a second fatal flaw.

Our Idol

For millennia, the inhabitants of earth had it all wrong. They were sure they were the center of their universe. Until Copernicus spoiled it. With his scientific evidence that, in fact, the sun was the center, and the earth revolved around the sun. So many were wrong about what was in the center of their universe.

It's a spiritual mistake we've all made. Putting one of the "planets" in our life in the center. Thinking the sun will revolve around it. When anyone or anything other than the God who made us is placed at the center of our life, it becomes our "idol."

Not a statue in the closet where we burn incense. But a person. An achievement. A career or a business. Our house or our image. Our body or our ability. Marriage or money. Even our son or daughter. Or our ministry.

Whenever someone or something takes God's place as the driver in our decisions, it has become what the First Commandment solemnly forbids: "You shall have no other gods before me" (Exodus 20:3). Another god.

There is only one throne in the human heart. The sign says, "Reserved for your Creator." But we continually marginalize Him and put our "precious" on the throne.

Until that god fails us. Which all false gods ultimately do.

In a curious account in the Old Testament, the pagan Philistines have captured Israel's storied ark of the covenant. At the time, it was the physical embodiment of the presence of God. The Philistines made the mistake of putting it in the temple of their fish god, Dagon. Poor Dagon. Every morning they kept finding him "fallen on his face on the ground before the ark of the LORD" (1 Samuel 5:3).

So it is with idols. And often we do not realize that we have made someone or something—even something noble—an idol. Until it "falls on its face."

If it has become sinfully important to us, God will allow us the heartache of losing it. To gain Him.

William Cowper, a hymnwriter of another generation, offered this plea to God:

> The dearest idol I have known...
> Help me to tear it from Thy throne
> And worship only Thee.

We've felt the pain of losing it. Now it's important not to miss the point of losing it. To put the "sun"—actually, the Son of God—in the center of our universe.

Then God can bless us with His good gifts. Knowing that now we'll worship the Giver, not the gift.

Sometimes, a picture tells the story. That's how it was with the photo my son texted me.

Dad and daughter were still at the pool where they were on vacation. Mom and two boys, ages seven and one, had just come back to their room. Mom asked the older brother to be in charge of his younger brother while she made a comfort stop.

We all knew younger brother was a handful—for two parents, let alone one seven-year-old brother. But Mom was only going to be gone briefly.

Now about the lemon meringue pie on the counter. At a glance, one would assume it was totally out of the reach of little brother. Oh, and older brother was immersed in a video game.

And the photo? A smushed lemon meringue pie on the floor and little brother with a fork that had somehow magically appeared. That's what Dad saw when he walked in.

Then came big brother's classic announcement: "Guess what, Daddy? I'm in charge here!"

Really. The mess told the story.

I wonder how many times my Heavenly Father has walked into a mess I've made and heard me say, "Guess what, Father? I'm in charge here!" To which He would have every right to say, "And it looks like it."

The fact is, we were never meant to be in charge. When we are, it sooner or later leads to a mess. But so many of us are, by nature, the most dangerous kind of freak of all. A control freak. Which turns the spotlight of God on a third fatal flaw where God wants to grow us.

Our Stubborn Control

You're driving down the highway when you see a hitchhiker up ahead. You don't usually stop, but something tells you that this time you should. You pull over and open the passenger door—and there stands Jesus. "Jesus, please—get in and ride with me."

His answer: "No."

"Why not, Jesus? I'd be honored to have You ride with me."

His answer says it all: "Because I don't ride. I drive."

He is God, and we're not. But somewhere in many of our lives, there is an area where we insist on driving. Trying to control our child, our spouse, our business, our finances, our future. As long as we're "in charge," we will ultimately ruin what we're trying to control.

So our loving Father intervenes to get our hands off the wheel. By causing what we're trying to control to spin out of control.

It's hard for us to see our control issue. Except through failure. And when we're in danger of losing whatever we've tried to control, we may finally consider the only way to peace and restoration.

Surrendering control. Of what we never should have been controlling in the first place. But that surrender is nothing to fear. Holding on to it is what we should fear.

And in surrendering, there is the sweet peace of a heavy burden finally being lifted off our back. Now the One who should be "in charge" is in charge.

THE BLESSING OF FAILURE

If we allow God to show us the lesson in the losing, then our failure can birth a new hope in us. Instead of leaving us devastated and defeated.

If we make redemptive choices in the rubble of our broken dream, we can emerge stronger than we've ever been before. And ready to pursue His dream, rather than our own.

And to do what Roy Riegels did.

He never dreamed that he would have a new first name before the Rose Bowl was over that January day in 1929. His University of California team was playing Georgia Tech in that celebrated football classic.

Playing center, he didn't expect to end up carrying the ball. But near halftime, Georgia Tech fumbled, and Roy Riegels grabbed it. Instinctively, he started running full speed toward the goal line. The wrong goal line. Georgia Tech's goal line.

Those guys chasing him were his own teammates, one of whom finally brought him down on the three-yard line. But that mistake ended up putting Georgia Tech in the position to score a two-point safety. At the end of the Rose Bowl, the final score was Georgia Tech, 8, University of California, 7.

And from that day to this, Roy has been known as Wrong Way Riegels. That's enough failure to make anybody lose hope.

It looked like it in the halftime locker room. Riegels was slumped in the corner. Until, much to his surprise, the coach told him he was starting second half. Roy objected. "Coach, I can't do it. I've ruined you, I've ruined myself, I've ruined the University of California. I couldn't face that crowd to save my life."

I love his coach's response: "Roy, get up and go back out there. The game is only half over." Roy Riegels went on to amaze the sportswriters with his stellar second-half performance. The following year, he earned All-American honors and was selected to be team captain.

As we have explored life's greatest hope killers, we have continued to come back to the fact that hope has a name. And His name is Jesus.

He's seen the mistakes. The sin. The wounds. The pain. He knows how beat up, how beat down you feel. How tempted you are to quit trying or to succumb to desperate measures.

But He is the Master of turning losses into learning. And failures into faith. Disappointments into determination. And crashes into character. He forgives. He restores. He rekindles. He rebuilds. He recycles hurt into hope.

He is the One who says, "Forget the former things; do not dwell on the past. See, I am doing a new thing! Now it springs up; do you not perceive it?" (Isaiah 43:18-19).

You may have been running the wrong way in the first half. But Jesus says, "Get up and go back out there. The game isn't over yet!"

And that's hope!

CHAPTER 9

HOPE WHEN YOUR HEALTH IS BROKEN

There is no pit so deep, that
God's love is not deeper still.

CORRIE TEN BOOM,
CONCENTRATION CAMP SURVIVOR

Mangers everywhere. That's always been our house at Christmas. My wife made sure there was a Nativity in every room. But there was no Nativity that December when she was in the cardiac critical care unit. She was fighting to recover from that shocking turn of events when she was in the cath lab for a heart stent to be installed. The cardiologist suddenly aborted the procedure, realizing that, with her arterial blockage, it could be fatal.

Shortly after, my son and I were told he needed to talk with us. His countenance told the story before he spoke a word. "If your wife doesn't have open-heart surgery immediately, she won't be here for Christmas. If she has the surgery, she can have maybe many more Christmases."

At 7:00 the next morning, she was in the operating room for open-heart surgery. The hours in the waiting room felt like days. The only reminder that Christmas was two weeks away was the high school carolers I heard in the lobby at lunchtime.

And then the love of my life was on a respirator, with tubes everywhere. It was hard seeing her like that.

During a stretch between visiting hours, I decided "we could use a little Christmas." I went to a nearby Christian bookstore to find a Nativity small enough that they might allow it in her otherwise bland room. I found it. I put it on her tray table. Today, it's at the head of our bed. All year long.

It's simple and small. Joseph, Mary, and baby Jesus in a tiny ceramic manger. With one word at the bottom.

Hope.

I needed that. Because when there's a medical crisis, hope takes a gut punch.

You go into a doctor's office with the sun shining and come out with a cloud over your future. At minimum, your life is going to change. You could be facing extended recovery, lifetime limitations, or ominous treatment. Or even the prospect of your life being over much sooner than you could have ever dreamed.

There are days when your "hope-ometer" reads pretty high. But those are punctuated by days when hope is replaced by fear, by discouragement, by loneliness, even by desperation or despair.

Broken health can mean broken hope. But, as with every one of life's hope robbers, hope is not determined by the situation. But by our choices.

And, as the title of a CNN article suggests, "Hope Can Help You Heal." The writer, Amanda Enayati, references the research of Jerome Groopman, as documented in his book *The Anatomy of Hope*. Groopman says:

Belief and expectation—the key elements of hope—can block pain by releasing the brain's endorphins and enkephalins, mimicking the effects of morphine. In some cases, hope can also have important effects on fundamental physiological processes like respiration, circulation and motor function.

So, while your health can steal your hope, apparently hope can help restore your health.

The CNN article went on to say that "Groopman's research showed that during the course of illness, belief and expectation—two mental states associated with hope—have an impact on the nervous system which, in turn, sets off a chain reaction that makes improvement and recovery more likely."

Broken health brings with it a flood of feelings that fluctuate day by day. Fear. Discouragement. Doubt. Worry. Uncertainty. Dread.

But hope? Not so much.

HOPE IN HEALTH STORMS

Hope is—and always must be—a choice. I've seen in real life the six anchors of hope in a medical "storm." In my wife's three life-threatening crises. Through health battles in our children over the years. In the gut-wrenching medical crises of grandchildren. And the shattering health challenges of good friends.

I have seen living proof that these anchors can move your health out of the driver's seat and put hope at the wheel. Whatever the diagnosis. Whatever the prognosis.

See Health Crises as Opportunities for Improved Vision

When my wife was driving, I had to read the road signs. By the time her nearsighted eyes could make out our exit sign, we might well be flying by it.

That all changed when she had Lasik surgery to improve her vision. Suddenly, she was reading the signs before I could. And noticing all kinds of beauty and detail never before seen along routes we had traveled many times. There was a constant exclamation of "Look at that!" Now she could see things she had never seen.

The ability to see what you couldn't see before—it can be a game changer when your health, or the health of someone you love, is in question. It is the first anchor of choosing hope.

When we're suddenly thinking about the bad things a health crisis could mean, it helps to realize the good things it can bring as well. By allowing God to use this disorienting time to help us open our eyes to what we may have missed.

The beautiful "Shepherd's Psalm," Psalm 23, includes five revealing words about His care for us. "The Lord is my shepherd...*He makes me lie down* in green pastures..." (verses 1-2, emphasis added).

I squirm a bit as I read "He makes me lie down." Because I know that is sometimes the only way He can get this hard-driving sheep to stop.

The Shepherd's most recent tool to slow me down has been four shoulder surgeries in one year. Nothing life-threatening, but certainly life-slowing. Especially for a guy who has gone all these years without surgery or hospitalization. I've always told people, "I visit hospitals. I don't stay." That changed this year.

But time to recover has been time to read. To think. To evaluate. To "see" more clearly. To look through a "wide-angle lens" at the big picture of my life and future.

I don't consider "makes me lie down" a punishment. It's an enforced opportunity. Because He makes us lie down in "green pastures." That's a spot that's good for a sheep in His care. A place of nourishment.

The next part of verse 2 says that "he leads me beside quiet waters, he refreshes my soul." That's what He did in the weeks following the devastating loss of my lifetime love. I needed to "lie down" and be led by "quiet waters" in order to see my upended life through His eyes.

Hope rises in a health battle when you see past the uncertainty to the opportunity. God wants to use this unexpected detour to enable you to actually see your life, not just do your life. I remember that years ago my wife said after a six-month convalescence from nearly fatal hepatitis, "God has used this to cleanse my schedule."

With no one expecting anything of her for months, she had a chance to look at her schedule and her commitments. And to start with a fresh piece of paper to rewrite some of the rhythms of her life.

A health sidelining is also an opportunity to see the people in your life differently. Their needs. Their value. Their weaknesses. Their strengths. In ways that are easy to miss in the day-to-day circus.

Recently, I've seen in medically embattled friends how the burden of broken health can become a major blessing. My friend Jay is way too young to have heard the doctor say he has a serious cancer. And that the battle ahead would involve painful and invasive treatment over months.

He's only in his thirties, with a beautiful wife, three young children, and a highly successful career. A great life—suddenly shrouded in a dark cloud. Because of one life-shattering word: *cancer*.

But his online journal of his journey has been laced with hope, not fear and despair. Oh, he's been honest about the struggle, the feelings that have no words. But somehow, hope has been winning. And spreading, through what he writes.

In part, because of what he's been able to see from the battle. For example, he writes: "The words cancer and chemo simply carry a weight that compels us to consider two things: 1) the totality of my life up to this point, and 2) how much life is left. I think it is normal for all of us to think about both the past and the future when we realize that we are not immortal."

His medical "all stop" has caused him to ask questions we all should ask: *How much of a difference has my life made so far, and will I still have time to make a lasting impact down the road?* To me, God very specifically designs and uses these moments to draw us to Himself as we confront the reality of dying someday.

For me, people like Jay are living proof that when you embrace a medical "lifequake" as a "Lasik season"—where you can see what you might not see any other way—you are choosing hope. And capturing the doctor's "bad news" as an opportunity to grow.

The chance to "improve your vision" suggests a second anchor for choosing hope when your health is in doubt.

Realize There's Something Bigger Going on Here

It's obvious from Jay's online posts soon after his diagnosis that he's found hope in that reality. He put it this way: "Please know that the unknown or uncertain will not lead us to panic or fear. We have a BIG God with BOLD plans and an even better purpose…My story is really just wrapped up in His story."

In Jay's life, in the health battles in our family, hope has come from looking to a very big God. With a very big Plan. Bigger than the chemo and the questions of the situation he can see. That hope is not just "positive thoughts." It's anchored hope. Anchored to promises made by a promise-keeping God:

> "I know the plans I have for you," declares the Lord, "plans
> to prosper you and not to harm you, plans to give you hope
> and a future" (Jeremiah 29:11).

No diagnosis, no prognosis can diminish the truth of that promise. Nor is there a cancer asterisk on God's assurance that "in all things

God works for the good of those who love him, who have been called according to his purpose" (Romans 8:28).

Now, on the other side of treatment and in a healthy recovery, Jay writes:

> So our cancer journey might look and feel like an unwelcome detour. Following months of reflection, reading and prayer, I'm convinced all of this was pre-planned for my good and a benefit for those who are vested by our side and in our circle.

From the beginning, Jay has chosen to embrace the Bigger Plan. To see this challenging detour as a planned detour. Planned by a good and loving God to accomplish His redemptive purposes.

When we choose to embrace that Plan, we are choosing hope.

When the kids were little, they looked a bit overwhelmed when you put a big serving of meat on their plate. But that was easily solved. Just cut it into small bites!

When our doctor told us that Karen would need six months of total bed rest at home to recover from her near-fatal bout of hepatitis, it felt overwhelming. My mind raced ahead to how I was going to do Mr. Mom for our three young children, lead our nonprofit organization, keep my many speaking and radio commitments, and maintain my extensive local youth ministry.

It had been over a month of our "new normal" when my pastor's wife blurted out her question: "Ron, we know how much you need and depend on Karen. How have you handled everything with her on the sidelines these past five weeks?"

With little hesitation, I just said, "I didn't handle five weeks. I handled thirty-five days." And that was really true. I couldn't have imagined doing five weeks—let alone six months—without Karen's partnership. What I could do was a Monday. Then a Tuesday, then a Wednesday. Cut that huge serving into bite-size chunks.

Because when a disease or injury or disability invades our lives, our tendency is to panic. Imagining all the "mights" and "coulds." Fast-forwarding to the most dire outcomes. Sinking at the thought of managing a month, a year—even a life—with this huge burden.

In the midst of the medical hits in our family over the year, I found a third anchor for choosing hope.

Do One Day at a Time

That simple saying, "One day at a time," is a lifesaver when broken health threatens to break your hope. And one word brings the seemingly "undoable" into the doable zone: *daily.*

From the Bible, "daily" appears to be the way we were created to do life. For example, "Praise be to the Lord, to God our Savior, who daily bears our burdens" (Psalm 68:19).

Jesus told His followers to "take up their cross daily" (Luke 9:23). God promises that "your strength will equal your days" (Deuteronomy 33:25). And the familiar Lord's Prayer requests that God "give us today our daily bread" (Matthew 6:11).

I know of no other way to approach an otherwise overwhelming medical hit than to take one day at a time. When I let myself run ahead to what the future might be, I run ahead of God's grace and strength—which are delivered fresh each day. Or, as the Bible says, "Because of the Lord's great love we are not consumed, for his compassions never fail. They are new every morning" (Lamentations 3:22-23).

File that word *daily* under "Hope."

Accept Your Situation as Your Assignment

I used to joke with my friend Howie, "Don't tell me what you're working on. If you did, I'm afraid you'd have to shoot me." That was my way of recognizing that much of his work was top-secret. It had something to do with satellites. Beyond that, forget it. His work was, to say the least, challenging.

But by far the biggest challenge of Howie's life was facing the treatment and likely prognosis of his aggressive cancer. For months, he knew he was dying. His body. Not his spirit.

Because he didn't see himself as a man dying of cancer. He was a man on a mission. And that mission was to spread hope to as many of his fellow cancer patients as possible. He was living another of those anchors for choosing hope when your body is under attack: Your situation is your assignment.

Howie's joy in the midst of suffering, Howie's hope with eternity looming, was rooted in a Person. Who Himself had conquered death. Jesus Christ. Whom the Bible describes as a "living hope" because of His "resurrection…from the dead" (1 Peter 1:3).

Since he was ready for eternity, he wanted others to be too. So day after day in that cancer ward, Howie was there praying with fellow patients, encouraging them, joyfully telling them about his Savior. The hospital ultimately recognized him for what he had become—the unofficial chaplain of the cancer ward.

The hospital had never seen a patient like Howie. He was a tireless dispenser of hope in one of life's most hope-starved situations. By the time he graduated to heaven, he had left an incalculable legacy of hope to cancer patients, their families, and to his doctors and nurses. He made such a difference that the hospital has now employed a full-time chaplain!

Howie was living one of the great choices of defiant hope: Live your life being hope for others. You're too busy helping others out of their pit to be drowning in your own.

When we own the reality of the bigger plan of God, we begin to see beyond our situation. To our assignment in the situation.

To those who, like Howie, have chosen to follow Jesus Christ, the assignment is clear: "We are...Christ's ambassadors" (2 Corinthians 5:20). An ambassador from our country is, in another country, the face and voice of the one who assigned him or her. In the same way, those who belong to Christ are to be His face and voice in their life situations.

Howie's situation changed dramatically from his high-tech office to a hospital cancer ward. But his assignment did not change. He was an ambassador of hope in both places. That's why the Bible directs believers to "always be prepared to give an answer to everyone who asks you to give the reason for the hope that you have" (1 Peter 3:15).

Our daughter did that in the darkest moments of her life—when the emergency room staff resigned themselves to the reality that they couldn't bring my wife back. In those awful moments, with her heart breaking, our daughter prayed for and with the medical staff in that room. And she shared the "reason for the hope" she had—her Jesus.

Even there, her situation was also her holy assignment.

A hospital bed...a wheelchair...a disability...a disturbing diagnosis...a deadly prognosis—all potentially crushing hope killers.

But your broken health can also position you to bring hope to broken hearts. They will listen to you. Because your condition has given you a platform from which to spread believable hope.

And, in the process, infuse a heavy dose of hope into your own embattled soul.

No matter how many more plays a football team would still like to run, they do not decide when the game is over. It's over when that big stadium clock registers zero. Time's up. Game over.

We can't see the divine game clock. That registers when our game is over. But the Bible reveals the powerful fact that each of our life clocks was set before we were born. By the One who gave us our life.

In a prayer recorded in the biblical Psalms, King David says, "You created my inmost being; you knit me together in my mother's womb. I praise you because I am fearfully and wonderfully made. Your works are wonderful" (Psalm 139:13-14). God's been there shaping my life since the second it began. When my life clock started running.

And His plan for me runs all the way to my final moment here. The psalmist's prayer continues: "All the days ordained for me were written in your book before one of them came to be" (Psalm 139:16).

That extraordinary revelation has given me another anchor for choosing hope for the time a health storm may obscure the sun.

Know You're Here Till Your Work Is Done

No disease will decide our destiny. No medical condition. No chart of survival rates.

Our Creator decided before I was born just how many "days" were "ordained for me." When someone dies, we tend to focus on the end of their life, reliving and rehashing their "cause of death." Sometimes even thinking of how it could have been avoided.

But the death certificate of a child of God could simply say under "cause of death"—"work done." I won't go Home a day before my work is done. I can't stay a day longer when my work is done.

To be sure, I didn't think my beloved Karen's work was done. With our grandchildren. With the hundreds of young women who looked to her as their "Mama Hutch." But that isn't mine to decide. The One who gave Karen her life determined its finish line.

So, as the Bible says, "There is a time for everything...a time to be born and a time to die" (Ecclesiastes 3:1-2). "A person's days are determined; you have decreed the number of his months and have set limits he cannot exceed" (Job 14:5).

So if and when the report from the doctor is grim, I know that neither a diagnosis nor prognosis will have the final word. A Heavenly Father who loves me determines my beginning and my end.

For me, for many, that's an anchor that enables us to choose hope over fear or despair. It's why my cancer-surviving friend Jay can say, "Jesus not only gives me significance for my life up to this point, but I am motivated more than ever to charge ahead and finish the race strong." And then, realizing there could still be questions ahead, "No matter how many miles remain."

There's a deep sense of peace in being able to say with the psalmist of old: "I trust in you, Lord; I say, 'You are my God.' My times are in your hands" (Psalm 31:14-15).

⸺⸺⸺

Sorry, but I can't help but chuckle at the announcement I've heard the flight attendant make before our commercial flight takes off: "Ladies and gentlemen, this is a destination check. We are flying to Atlanta today. If you are planning on another destination, this would be a good time to deplane."

That just makes me smile. The chuckle has come in those rare instances when a passenger has actually gotten up and gotten off at that point. Amid the bemused or belittling stares of the rest of the plane. I'll stop laughing the day I'm the one getting off.

Actually, a destination check is a good idea. Especially when it's our destination on the other side of our last heartbeat. It's the one destination you don't want to be wrong about.

And when you know there's nothing to fear beyond death, it extracts so much of the fear and anxiety from a medical crisis.

Secure Your Destination

Troubled. One of the words that describe the torrent of emotions triggered by bad news from the doctor.

In His final hours before His crucifixion, Jesus used that word in one of His most treasured promises: "Do not let your hearts be troubled…My Father's house has many rooms…I am going there to prepare a place for you…that you also may be where I am" (John 14:1-3).

As the tide was turning in Jay's war with cancer, he wrote about having a very heavy heart. "My good friend Jim passed away yesterday after battling cancer for the last two years." Jay continued, "I was most inspired by Jim when he talked about his ultimate destination with conviction."

Jim told him, "I'm looking forward to heaven. I think it's going to be awesome. I'm excited to be a citizen of a place where there is no suffering. I really hope they have donuts, by the way."

Jim had a faith that enabled him to face the end of his life with peace, with confidence. With hope. Hope that even defies the dark passage of death. As King David wrote centuries ago, "Though I walk through the valley of the shadow of death, I will fear no evil; for You are with me" (Psalm 23:4 NKJV).

HOPE THAT ISN'T

The Thirty Mile Fire was one of those Western forest fires that suddenly roared to life and turned on the heroic men and women who were there to fight it. For many of those firefighters, their foil tents were the difference between life and death.

But four rookie firefighters decided to try to escape the flames, believing the road would lead them to safety. It was a fatal mistake. The road turned out to be a dead end.

When I first read that story, I thought, "What an awful tragedy. The road they thought would lead them to safety was a dead-end road." Then, remembering many conversations I've had with people about our ultimate destination, I thought of the Scripture verse that says, "There is a way that appears to be right, but in the end it leads to death" (Proverbs 14:12).

Apparently, we can think we are going to heaven and be fatally wrong. Eternally wrong.

Jesus's disciples inquired about the right road when Jesus told them He was preparing a place where people could be with Him forever. One of the disciples said, "Lord, we don't know where you are going, so how can we know the way?" (John 14:5).

That question elicited what is perhaps the boldest statement Jesus ever made: "I am the way and the truth and the life. No one comes to the Father except through me" (John 14:6).

It is a claim that stirs many reactions. But clearly a claim that needs to be considered. If it is true, it means many ways "that appear to be right" are dead-end roads. It means that no religion is the way, even Christian religion. It means the way is a Person.

It is the only Person who paid the price for the sin of our life to be forgiven. Our lifetime of pushing God to the edge and running a life that He was supposed to run separates us from Him. If we're honest, we can almost feel the wall between us and God. That feeling is right. As the Bible says, "Your iniquities have separated you from your God" (Isaiah 59:2).

If we come to our last breath, and that wall is still there, the Bible says it will be there forever. We can't get into heaven with our sin.

Sin carries a death penalty. And no amount of religion or goodness can pay a death penalty. No, somebody has to die.

And Somebody did. I was blown away to discover that Jesus "bore our sins in His own body on the tree" (1 Peter 2:24 NKJV). That "tree" is the cross where God's Son absorbed all the hell for all my sin.

Nobody has ever loved me like that. Nobody ever could.

So Jesus's audacious statement that He alone is the way to make heaven our destination is not audacious at all. It is His loving invitation to be with Him forever. And He is the Way because the only One who can forgive my sins is the One who died for my sins.

And the only One who can give me eternal life is the only One who ever proved He has it. And that proof was an empty tomb on Easter morning where history records He conquered death. He is our anchored hope of heaven. Any other hope is hope that isn't.

We cannot know the day or the way of our death. A lingering disease may bring us into eternity. Or a sudden stroke or heart attack. Or a drunk driver crossing the center line. A storm, a fire, a flood.

But we can know where we will be 30 seconds after that last heartbeat. Jesus left no doubt: "I am the resurrection and the life. The one who believes in me will live, even though they die" (John 11:25-26).

Ultimate hope, ultimate peace is knowing you're ready for eternity, whenever and however it comes.

For my precious Karen, it came suddenly. But years before, she had pinned all her hopes for heaven on Jesus, as I have. There was no mystery about where she was the moment she left us. She was, in the Bible's words, "away from the body, at home with the Lord" (2 Corinthians 5:8). This is a hope so defiant, so sure that it defies death itself.

So, standing by her fresh grave, I could say with full assurance, "See you soon, baby."

And I will.

CHAPTER 10

HOPE WHEN YOUR PAST IS BROKEN

Do not dwell on the past.
See, I am doing a new thing!

Isaiah 43:18-19

It seems like it's there after every flight. On the baggage carousel. We passengers keep watching for the chute to spit out our trusty bag. And we eagerly claim it and head for the exit.

But if you happen to be the lucky winner whose bag comes out last, you'll see it. The mystery suitcase. Making its forty-third trip around. No one has claimed it. No one ever does. It just keeps going around and around.

Sadly, many of us have baggage like that. Emotional baggage. Life baggage. A suitcase full of painful memories. And it just keeps coming back around. And we just keep letting it.

In our suitcase are the tormenting memories of being abused. Or abandoned…neglected…bullied…beaten. Our heart carries deep wounds from betrayal or injustice. Being burned by family or friends. By an employer, by a church.

Sadly, the pain of our past keeps leaking poison into our present. All that buried hurt doesn't stay buried. It morphs into bitterness and anger that infects our close relationships. It robs us of our ability to trust, to feel safe, to give and receive love. And all too often, that painful baggage spawns unexplainable and recurring bouts with depression. Sometimes dangerous depression.

When we allow the pain of our past to live in our present, it darkens part of our heart. Which then releases the past to become a powerful hope robber today, and for all those tomorrows.

Our broken past is draining our hope. And carrying us into a broken future.

Unless we make the choices that lead us to a hope that frees us from the hurt. They are courageous choices. But they are liberating choices.

I was on the football field with our high school team. My 12-year-old son was on an adjacent field, playing a pickup game of football with some friends.

I'll never forget the scene of him walking toward me, holding his arm. An arm that was obviously broken in multiple places. Mr. Tough Junior High Guy was trying desperately not to cry—but the pain was excruciating.

In the emergency room, the orthopedist confirmed a break so bad we could actually see it in the twisted shape of his arm. The doctor set to work to reset the damaged bones.

When a parent sees their child in almost unbearable pain, they wish for the impossible: "I wish we could trade places so I could take the pain for him." Instead, we just had to watch our son suffer through it.

Theoretically, he could have avoided all that pain. "It hurts too much to fix it. I'll just leave it broken." In which case he wouldn't be playing the guitar. Or carrying his young children. Or navigating ATMs and drive-through restaurants. Or managing a thousand other life situations where a functioning arm is essential equipment.

The choice that meant hope for the future was a painful one. But a temporary one. He could either choose short-term pain and have the use of his arm for the rest of his life. Or let the temporary pain keep him from a functioning arm the rest of his life.

FREEDOM FROM LIFE'S BAGGAGE

The four choices that set us free from the baggage of a lifetime involve some pain. Temporary pain. For permanent gain. I had pain from my recent shoulder surgery. But by enduring that for a short time, I can have a shoulder that works for the rest of my life.

My work has brought me into the lives of many broken people. I've had the sorrow of seeing some refuse to open that suitcase and unpack it once and for all. And watch them continue to make the hurtful choices that only compound the pain.

And I've had the privilege of walking with others through the struggles of dealing with what's broken inside them. And then watching them blossom and flourish afterward as they are able to run without their lifetime baggage.

The ones who came out free and whole have made four hope choices to heal a broken past.

Face It

We'd rather flee it. That's why so many just keep stuffing their pain. And look instead to temporary pain relievers—a bottle, a drug, an affair, busyness, bad relationships. Never a cure. Just occasional relief. But often with "sedatives" that end up causing more pain.

The problem with denial is it never changes reality. The ticking time bomb inside continues ticking. Until one day it erupts in a volcano of desperation, depression, or rage.

The only way to be free is to drag what's been stuffed in the closet out into the light. With it probably kicking and screaming all the way. But just beyond the battle is freedom. As Jesus said in one of His most-quoted statements, "You will know the truth, and the truth will set you free" (John 8:32).

I've been intrigued with a particular passage of Scripture that addresses the darkness in our soul. It begins with the fact that "God is light; in him there is no darkness at all" (1 John 1:5). Then it promises, "If we walk in the light, as he is in the light, we have fellowship with one another, and the blood of Jesus, his Son, purifies us from all sin" (verse 7).

I see reasons to finally stop running from the pain of my past—whether from what I've done or what others have done to me. Reasons to unlock that closet door and let the dark monster of the past out.

To "walk in the light" with "no darkness at all," means dragging the dark secrets out into the light. So there it is—the big, ugly monster of hurt that I've stuffed forever. He makes a lot of noise because he can't stand being out in the light.

The payoff for taking the risk of facing it? First, healing in your close relationships—"fellowship with one another." Because it's usually the poison from our past that leaks into our marriage, our kids, our friends, our coworkers. Facing it is the first step to stopping the contamination from the toxic waste dump inside us.

The other payoff for facing our hurt and our wrong choices is healing in our relationship with God. We face it. That opens up the dark places for God to heal what's broken and forgive what's wrong.

Our son (of broken-arm fame) was pioneering a youth outreach among Native Americans on a remote reservation. That part he had planned. He hadn't planned on this Native young woman stealing his heart. (And ultimately becoming our much-loved daughter!)

But taking her on dates was a bit of a challenge. In order to get to her house, he had to endure this deeply rutted, teeth-rattling reservation road that went through open range. Where roaming cattle defied cars as they sped down the road. We often joked that every time our son went on a date, three jackrabbits were no more. They felt free to pop up anytime on that road.

It was a pretty harrowing trip. There was another road our son could have taken. It was paved and smooth and easy to navigate. One problem: The destination he wanted (the house of his beloved) wasn't on the easy road. It could only be reached by enduring the bumpy road.

The road to denial and buried pain appears to be the easy road (for a while). But the only road to hope, to healing, to freedom is the bumpy road of facing it. It's a courageous choice. But it's the liberating choice.

Once you've courageously faced what's been stuffed, you're ready for the second choice that replaces hurt with hope.

Fix It

We had a piano to move. I remember when my dad helped move a piano when I was little. And that particular exercise has been associated with another word ever since then. *Hernia*. It wasn't long after lifting that piano that he had to have hernia surgery.

So one thing about moving a piano was tattooed on my brain: Get plenty of outside help. Because it's just too heavy to lift alone.

Just like the pain of our past. We need outside assistance to lift it. What's happened to us in the past is just too heavy to lift alone.

So the second hope choice is another step of courage. To tell someone about what you may have told no one for years. But not just any someone.

There are people who've walked this trail with many others. Who have spent years training for sensitive times, just like this. Counselors. Some pastors.

In the past, many have remained enslaved by the chains of their past because of fear. Or pride. That kept them from reaching out. From finally putting their pain into words. From digging up what's been buried and toxic for so long.

In the Bible's wise words, "Two are better than one...if either of them falls down, one can help the other up. But pity anyone who falls and has no one to help them up...Though one may be overpowered, two can defend themselves" (Ecclesiastes 4:9-10,12).

If the "two" includes someone skilled at asking liberating questions, discovering a way forward and providing emotional support, you really can fix what's broken. The "two are better" verses end with this somewhat curious conclusion: "A cord of three strands is not quickly broken." First, it was two. Suddenly, it's three.

For me, that third strand is the one that makes all the difference. Because when Jesus is by your side as you confront your past, you have the greatest love and support in the universe with you.

And He really gets the wounds of life in a world like ours. He's been here. And He was "despised and rejected by mankind, a man of suffering, and familiar with pain" (Isaiah 53:3).

No one understands what you've suffered like Jesus. But He doesn't just empathize. "He heals the brokenhearted and binds up their wounds" (Psalm 147:3).

A counselor can perform the delicate emotional surgery needed to diagnose and treat the wounds inside. The Savior can heal them.

So when you finally open that closet door and let the monster out, you are not alone. Jesus is there to face it with you.

They call it the "three-legged race." They should call it the two-klutz race.

They tie your left leg to your partner's right leg. And then you get to run the little race course like that. I thoroughly expected to be dragged on the ground to the finish line by a very frustrated teammate. I actually made it standing up. With a very frustrated teammate.

I'm convinced that even an Olympic track star would look like a klutz running like that. You just can't run well when you're tied to someone else!

Sadly, many of us are trying to run while emotionally tied to the last person we'd choose to run with. The person who abused us. Who betrayed or abandoned or wounded us. In a sense, the one who hurt us is always with us.

Because we haven't made the third choice to release us from a broken past and replace it with hope.

Forgive It

Just reading that word can elicit a visceral response. "Forgive? After what they did to me? I can't. I won't."

This step toward emotional freedom is arguably the hardest and most costly. But not nearly as hard, not nearly as costly as harboring the bitterness. Running tied to the person who hurt you for the rest of your life. Replaying over and over what they did to you.

Unforgiveness takes up lodging in a wounded heart. And usually has a list of understandable reasons for being there. The hurt is real and deep. And the memories pursue us relentlessly, continually dragging the worst of our past into our present.

Unforgiveness doesn't stay unforgiveness. It grows, silently but surely, into bitterness. Which is a poison that ultimately afflicts the people we love.

The Bible explains why: "See to it that no one falls short of the grace of God and that no bitter root grows up to cause trouble and defile many" (Hebrews 12:15).

First of all, the thought of missing the grace of God is somewhere I don't want to go. How does God's grace get blocked from entering my heart? Bitterness is there. And apparently, God's grace and our bitterness cannot coexist in the same heart.

And bitterness "grows up." So if you don't let it go, you're letting it grow. And when it does, it "causes trouble" in other relationships and "defiles many." It's relationship poison. And usually hurts the people we love far more than that person whose wound planted the bitter seed.

There is only one way to break the chains forged by the wrong done to you. Make the third choice that turns your heart from hurt to hope: Forgive it.

Until you forgive, you're hopelessly tied to the one(s) who hurt you. Unless you forgive, you will have cancer in your soul.

And, like hope, forgiveness isn't a feeling. It's a choice.

There are countless reasons we can cite for not forgiving. There is one big reason the Bible gives to forgive. "Bear with each other and forgive one another if any of you has a grievance against someone…" (Colossians 3:13). Then comes the bottom line that leaves me defenseless: "Forgive as the Lord forgave you."

I know how the Lord forgave me. Absolutely not because I deserved it. Not after putting myself on the throne of my life. A throne that rightly belongs only to the One who gave me my life. My selfishness, my pride, my anger, my lies, my dark secrets, my hijacking of my life from my Creator—so horrific it took God's Son, butchered on a cross, to pay for it.

For God, forgiving me was a choice. An unspeakably expensive choice.

So how can I, who has received so much forgiveness from a perfect God, refuse to give it to someone who has wronged me?

Unforgiveness looks at my wounder and sees someone who hurt me deeply. Forgiveness looks at my wounder and sees someone Jesus thought was worth dying for. And even sees a person who was probably someone else's victim. Whose untreated wound turned the wounded into a wounder. Because hurt people hurt people.

My decision to forgive is not a decision to excuse the wrong done. It is a decision to treat the one who hurt me not as they treated me, but as Jesus treated me. Unconditional forgiveness.

And you are not alone when you choose to let it go. You can go to the Great Forgiver and ask for His grace when you don't have it to give. You let His forgiveness fill your heart. He waits only for you to make the choice to forgive. Realizing that forgiving is not an event.

It's a process. That can only start with the forgiving choice. The hope choice.

I know it's possible. I have seen it happen in the darkest of situations, with even the most appalling abuse.

For more than 25 years, my wife and I have had the privilege of knowing, loving, and serving with some amazing Native American young people. Traveling with them in multitribal teams to over a hundred reservations, we have seen them bring hope to some of the most hope-starved communities on the continent.

They are unlikely messengers for a message of hope. Many, if not most, of the young men and women on the team have heartbreaking stories of violence and abuse of all kinds. And most of their stories include how rare it is to find someone who had a father who was a father. Often, he is one of the greatest sources of their pain. Addiction to alcohol and/or drugs has been the "normal" they know—along with the violence, abuse, and neglect that usually accompanies it.

Unlikely hope carriers. But over and over, I have watched how their stories of hope have captured the pain-hardened hearts of reservation young people. It is a hope they say is anchored in Jesus Christ. Who has forgiven their sin and brought healing to seemingly irreparable brokenness.

I think of Marcy. Betrayed—sexually assaulted—by her mother's boyfriend, whom she trusted implicitly. From that wound came a chain of self-destructive choices on Marcy's part. Gangs. Fighting. Lashing out at everyone. Heart hardened. Doing drugs.

Dealing drugs. And finally, one night, she held a gun to her own head to end her pain.

That was the night Jesus intervened and captured her heart. Sometime later, I was with Marcy when she sensed God saying, "You'll never be free until you forgive." There was a battle that night. And tons of tears. Until she finally, with God's help, made the choice. To forgive the man who had virtually ruined her life.

A process began that night and grew as Marcy worked through the layers of hurt with caring counselors. Her choice to forgive triggered a near-miraculous chain of events in her family. Beginning with a real relationship with the mother who had told Marcy she wished she had never been born. Who, when Marcy was violated by her mother's boyfriend, sided with him rather than with her own daughter.

A lot to forgive. But Jesus is a powerful Savior. The emotionally liberated Marcy has so affected her family that hopelessly broken relationships have been healed. In many ways, Marcy has a family for the first time in her life.

And it all started with a choice to forgive. Not just for her. It is the story of one after another of our treasured "sons and daughters" in Native America. Forgiven. Then forgiving. Then free.

It's a big deal when a child gets old enough to have their car seat turned around. Until they hit certain weight and age milestones, it's safest for their kiddie seat to face backward as a safety precaution. But then, one day, everything changes.

Instead of looking where they've already been, they get to look at where they're going!

In a sense, that's what happens when you forgive. Your fixation on the hurt of the past turns to a focus on hope for your future. In the hope-filled words of the Bible:

> Forget the former things; do not dwell on the past. [Turn your seat around!] See, I am doing a new thing! Now it springs up; do you not perceive it? (Isaiah 43:18-19).

Part of that new thing is an exciting possibility that would have been unthinkable in the shadowland of unforgiveness. It is the fourth choice on the road from "victim" to hope.

Free Others

In Dr. Seuss's immortal *The Grinch Who Stole Christmas*, the grumpy Grinch, who lives on the mountain, is royally irritated by the niceness of the people of Whoville in the valley. He is determined to change that by stealing all their Christmas presents during the night before Christmas.

But the next morning, he is amazed to hear the Whoville folks joyfully singing songs of Christmas. And their unselfish joy does something the Grinch could never have imagined.

Dr. Seuss says of the Grinch, "His heart grew three sizes that day." And changed the Grinch forever.

That's what can happen to a human heart that has faced, fixed, and forgiven the great hurts of a lifetime. And now there is room for a new compassion to be born in that liberated heart. A compassion that now can see and feel the brokenness of others in a hurting world.

I am deeply moved as I see Native young people, who were once defined by their hurt, now defined by their hope. And wanting to help others experience the freedom they've found.

Freedom from the hurt inflicted by others. Healed through forgiving.

Freedom from the hurt resulting from their own sinful choices. Healed by being forgiven as they bring all that baggage to the cross where Jesus died to pay for it. And they leave it all there.

There's nothing like giving hope to grow hope in your own heart. Focusing on your pain is focusing on yourself. Once those chains are broken, you can begin to be hope for other "victims." And they'll listen. Because you've been there.

THE UGLY STAIN MIRACLE

It happened in a little seaside café in Scotland. Two fishermen were having one of those "Can you top this?" conversations about who had brought in the largest fish.

One of them tried to describe his "big one" with a sweeping gesture of his hand. Which, unfortunately, sent a full teapot crashing against the wall. And leaving an ugly brown stain.

The disgusted owner said he would now have to repair the whole wall to get rid of that stain. A lone man at another table asked if he could have a few minutes to work on that stain. "You may not need to repair it," he said. With nothing to lose, the owner let him proceed.

The man pulled out some paints and brushes and began to use the wall as his canvas. He began to sketch around the stain, coloring, shaping, shading. Soon an image began to emerge—a deer with an impressive rack of antlers. It was a minor masterpiece!

Little did folks know that the man with the brushes just happened to be the famous wildlife painter E.H. Landseer. Who, with his great skill, demonstrated that you don't have to settle for an ugly stain simply being erased or covered. It can be transformed into a thing of beauty.

That's the miracle Jesus has been doing with pain-stained, sin-stained lives for 2,000 years. Transforming what once was ugly and depressing into a thing of beauty.

A broken past can, in the hands of Jesus, become hope for a hurting world.

CHAPTER 11

MAKING THINGS WORSE

May your choices reflect your hopes, not your fears.

NELSON MANDELA

You're new to America. You're here from another country, but you studied English in school. If only Americans talked the way it's taught. We talk in slang and idioms that will totally confuse this newcomer.

Take the phrase I just heard again the other day, describing a man who is messing up his own chances for a promotion. "Yeah, he really shot himself in the foot." I'm that newcomer, listening to that. I know what all those words mean. Poor fellow. What hospital is he in?

Strangely, his foot is fine. He's not in the hospital. There was no gun; there were no bullets.

There was before we changed the meaning. "Shooting yourself in the foot" actually goes back to World War I, when it was a well-known survival tactic. An American aviator in the British Army was hospitalized from a plane crash. He reported that "the fellow in the bed next to mine had shot himself in the foot to avoid going into battle. A lot of them did that, but why they picked their own feet is beyond me. It's a nasty place, full of small bones."

SHOOTING OURSELVES IN THE FOOT

Today, you don't need a gun to shoot yourself in the foot. Because the phrase has morphed to mean "to cause oneself difficulty; to be the author of one's own misfortune."

By that definition, most of us have "shot ourselves in the foot." In many cases, making bad things worse.

Sadly, we are most prone to making those kinds of choices at some of the hardest times in our lives. When you lose someone or something you really love or really need—one of your life anchors—you're suddenly in uncharted territory. Unsure of which way to go.

I remember vividly a deep feeling of lostness when I suddenly lost my Karen, my treasure. I only knew life with Karen. I had no idea what life without Karen was.

Those same feelings of "What do I do now?" are part of the shock of many of life's losses. Suddenly, you're out of work. Or facing financial crisis. Or the collapse of your marriage. A breakup. A divorce—yours or your parents'. There's bad news from the doctor. Or a life-changing injury or disaster.

And unfortunately, we're so prone to come up with the wrong answer to "What do I do now?" We had no choice about the life "hammer" that hit us. But what we do to deal with the loss is totally our choice.

That's when we may "shoot ourselves in the foot." Making choices that make bad things worse. Compounding the pain of our loss with decisions that cause us to lose even more.

As I've been there with countless people in their time of loss, I've seen it happen all too often. Bad news, followed by bad choices.

Most of this book has been about how to make the choices that lead to hope. But there's an important flip side. How to avoid the choices that lead to more hurt.

I've lived it. I've seen it. Four mistakes we're prone to make when hope just walked out the door. Mistakes that almost never end well.

The Fear Factor

First, deciding out of FEAR.

Financial fear that causes us to try to fix the problem by going into more debt. Fear of losing our marriage or a rebellious child—so we become a control freak and push them even farther away. Fear of being alone—so we run into a relationship that ends up making us even lonelier.

So often, what we do for relief only ends up as regret. And compounded sadness. And even more lost hope.

There's a reason "fear not" is one of the Bible's most oft-repeated commands. Fear usually distorts our judgment and ignores long-term consequences.

Some of my most costly decisions—or indecisions—have been motivated by fear. Failing to confront someone because I was afraid of what I might lose. In the end, I lost a lot more because I let it go and let it grow.

One of the tragic ironies is how fear-based responses usually backfire. By acting out of fear, we often cause the very outcome we feared would happen.

Right now, I know a mother who is very afraid her rebellious son is headed for the same kind of destructive choices she made as a teenager. He's in an unhealthy relationship that she fears is taking him on a spiritually dangerous road. So she's trying to take away every possible way he could communicate with the girl.

I've seen this drama so many times before. By his mother cutting off contact, he will resort to more desperate measures to be with this girl. By trying to keep them apart, she will likely drive them together. The very thing she fears.

By trying to control, we ultimately lose the person. By going for a quick fix, we end up in deeper trouble. By freaking out, we make things even worse.

Fear makes us vulnerable to decisions we will later regret. I'm so thankful for promises like this from God—promises that say, "Breathe, Ron. I've got this": "I am the Lord your God, who takes hold of your right hand and says to you, 'Do not fear; I will help you'" (Isaiah 41:13).

He did that on the day of the greatest loss of my life. He's been keeping that promise every day since.

Blinded by Anger

A second hurt-compounding mistake we're prone to make is deciding out of ANGER.

God speaks to this pretty bluntly: "You all must be quick to listen, slow to speak, and slow to get angry. Human anger does not produce the righteousness God desires" (James 1:19-20 NLT).

My short version: You don't do anything right when you're mad.

In fact, some of the synonyms we use for *angry* are revealing in themselves. *Mad*, for example. *Burned up. Blew his top. Lost it.* We know the actions and decisions carried out in anger are almost always destructive.

So, God warns us: "Stop being angry! Turn from your rage! Do not lose your temper—it only leads to harm" (Psalm 37:8 NLT). And, "a hot-tempered person commits all kinds of sin" (Proverbs 29:22 NLT).

But when something or someone we have put our hopes in lets us down or leaves, we may lash out in anger. Wounded animals do that. At times, wounded humans do too.

Generally, the more heat there is, the less light there is. We're blinded by anger. And decisions made then are bound to leave wounds on others and self-inflicted wounds on ourselves. What's done in a moment of anger can create a lifetime of regret. Again, further compounding the pain and crushing hope.

Desperate for Love

Five thousand dating websites! Based on the law of supply and demand, there is obviously a massive demand for romance!

There are the high-profile sites like eharmony.com. And match.com, that advertises "more people, more relationships, your chance for love." If you've had 50 or more birthdays, there's ourtime.com.

There are niche sites too. Like farmersonly.com. If you have or like a beard, how about Bristlr.com? Or Sizzl.com that pairs you up based on bacon preferences? And there's always Gluten-freeSingles.com. Even dateacowboy.com.

The world's love lottery is big business! But hiding beneath the abundance of these websites is evidence of a lot of loneliness. And that's understandable in light of so many broken families, broken promises, and broken hearts.

We pin a lot of our hopes on relationships. Especially someone to love and who will love us. But as time goes by, that hope can start turning to hurt. And disillusionment. And sometimes desperation.

And that sets us up for the third mistake we can make that makes a bad time even worse: deciding out of LONELINESS.

Lonely-driven choices often come from lost love. Or love that never was. A shattered marriage. A romantic breakup—which, in these days of social media, can just suddenly be announced by changing your status from "in a relationship" one day to "single" the next. The heartache of loneliness hits, as well, with the death of your lifetime love. Or each birthday that passes with you still single.

It pains me to see, over and over again, people making ultimately hurtful choices in times like that. The choice to "settle." Which the dictionary says is "to accept in spite of incomplete satisfaction." And more sobering, "to sink gradually to the bottom."

"Anybody is better than nobody"—maybe for a short time. But I have listened to the heartache of both men and women who "settled." Who, after the initial exhilaration of having someone, know they're now stuck with the wrong someone.

Loneliness can blind us to weaknesses, incompatibilities, and danger signs that will later define the relationship. It can cause us to give sex to get or keep love—only to end up used instead of loved. Or to convince ourselves that—as one young woman told me—"this is all I can get." "All I can get" got lost before long.

My sister-in-law is one of the most selfless, generous, and caring people I know. Her life has blessed every member of our family—and many others. She's always been single. Not for want of opportunities to marry. She just refused to "settle." As she says, "I'd rather have no one than the wrong someone!"

She's not without love, though. She has been like a second mother to all three of our children and all nine of our grandchildren. And, believe me, they love her! Beyond that, she long ago opened her heart to the deepest, most fulfilling love in the universe—to the One who loved her enough to die for her. To Jesus.

One powerful defense against the mistakes we make for love is to be able to recognize what genuine love really looks like. And our Creator has given us a wonderful description to guide us:

Love is patient and kind. Love is not jealous or boastful or proud or rude. It does not demand its own way. It is not irritable, and it keeps no record of being wronged. It does not rejoice about injustice but rejoices whenever the truth wins out. Love never gives up, never loses faith, is always hopeful, and endures through every circumstance (1 Corinthians 13:4-7 NLT).

When you are anchored by a relationship with the One who will always love you like that, you can avoid a relationship that ends up as regret. A romantic "dream" that becomes a nightmare.

There's something lonelier than not being married. It's being married to the wrong person. That is the loneliest lonely of all.

"Are We There Yet?"

It's the cry from a thousand backseats. It certainly was from ours. And now our grown children get to hear it from their backseat. I'm smiling.

"Are we there yet?" It appears to be commonly believed among children that frequency of asking will somehow make the car grow wings. No, we're not there yet. You'll be among the first to know.

I can't help but wonder if that's how we sound to God at times: "When are we going to be there? This is taking too long!"

"My prayer isn't being answered." "My problem isn't getting solved." "The money still hasn't come." "I'm still single." "My spouse is never going to change." "It's been so long—this kid is hopeless."

As more time passes and we're not "there yet," we edge toward a fourth mistake that often ends in more pain and lasting regrets: deciding out of IMPATIENCE.

So often we're like the pastor whose secretary walked in on him pacing back and forth in his office. When she asked why, he responded curtly, "Because I'm in a hurry...and God isn't!"

That's usually a pretty fair description of me and God. I'm in a hurry. He's taking His time. Fulfilling His promise that "he has made everything beautiful in its time" (Ecclesiastes 3:11). But His time is almost always later than my time.

Babies take nine months to develop before they're ready to take on this world. Some come sooner. A lot sooner. And while a woman may have had enough pregnancy by six months, she would never wish her baby came then. The baby would be premature. We don't want that baby to be born until he or she is full term.

Sadly, when we're hurting from whom or what we've lost, we're prone to run right past God to try to make things happen. And, in our impatience, we end up with an unhealthy preemie instead of God's best.

That's what happened to Moses. He was a Jewish boy, providentially brought into the family of Pharaoh, the king of Egypt. As an adult, he began to seethe over the brutal enslavement of his people, the Jews. Apparently, he had a sense that he was God's man to rescue his people.

But he couldn't wait. He tried to start the liberation by killing an abusive Egyptian slave master. "Moses thought that his own people would realize that God was using him to rescue them, but they did not" (Acts 7:25). He was forced to flee for his life. To the wilderness. Where this prince of Egypt lived as a herder of sheep for 40 years.

He tried to make things happen—and made a mess instead.

Just like us when we act because we're impatient. We run ahead of God's perfectly timed plan and end up in more debt…in more trouble…more pain…more lonliness. With our loss compounded by a mess of our own making.

Moses had the right idea. He was God's choice to deliver his people. But not yet. Moses couldn't wait for God's time. Moses wanted it now. Just like many of us.

Isaac's wife, Rebekah, made a similar mistake in trying to force something God had promised. When her fraternal twin sons were born, Esau arrived first. His brother, Jacob, actually landed with his hand grasping Esau's heel. Normally, as the firstborn, Esau would inherit the leadership and much of the wealth of the family. But God had promised Rebekah prenatally that "the older will serve the younger" (Genesis 25:23).

Years later, when it looked as if Papa Isaac was dying, Rebekah began to panic. Time was almost up, and the father's blessing still rested with Esau. Esau was the hairy, "Field and Stream" hunter—Dad's favorite. While Jacob was the "Good Housekeeping" homebody chef— Mom's favorite.

With Isaac deteriorating each day, Rebekah decided God needed a little help keeping His promise. Putting animal skins on Jacob so he would feel and smell like Esau to a father whose eyesight was failing, she told her boy to pretend he was his brother. And it worked! They succeeded in deceiving Isaac into giving the coveted blessing to Jacob.

Nice work, Rebekah. You got what you wanted. But in her impatience, she had sown to the wind and would reap the whirlwind. When Esau learned of the deception—and all he had lost—he swore, "I will kill my brother Jacob" (Genesis 27:41).

Jacob had to flee for his life. He was in virtual exile for 14 years, living in mortal fear of his brother. And himself cheated by an unscrupulous uncle out of what he had earned. P.S.— Isaac recovered and lived 20 more years!

Rebekah's impatience and inability to wait for God came at a very high price. Her family was ripped apart, her older son wanted to kill her younger son—and by the time Jacob could return home, Rebekah had died. She never got to see her beloved son again.

Such a sad story of impatience trying to make things happen, and again, making a mess instead. But those stories aren't just in the Bible. So many of us have written our own story called "Mission Impatient." A story that doesn't end with "they lived happily ever after."

"Oh, what needless pain we bear." Those words from an old hymn describe the consistent cost of deciding out of impatience. When it's God's time and God's way, "his way is perfect" (2 Samuel 22:31).

But the hardest room in God's "house" is the waiting room. But that's where He builds faith. That's where He grows our faith from trusting in an outcome to trusting Him. While we wait, He is getting us ready for His answer and His answer ready for us. When we rush it, we ruin it.

The Hebrew words used for hope in the Old Testament each link hope to waiting: *Tiqwa* means "to await, to expect, to hope for." *Yachal* literally speaks of an object to be waited for. It's actually the word for being in labor and waiting in painful expectation.

I'm reminded of the days leading up to the birth of our daughter's first child. My wife was lovingly coaching our girl on what to expect. "The pain is going to get to a point where you're saying, 'That's it! I can't take it anymore!' Hang in there, honey. That's when the baby will come!"

As we feel like giving up…as it hurts so bad we feel like we can't go on—there's our Heavenly Father saying, "Hang in there. What you've been waiting for is almost here!"

Yes, hope is inextricably bound together with waiting. And God's best is always worth the wait.

God's Old Testament prophet Micah has given us the blueprint for getting God's best: "But as for me, I watch in hope for the Lord, I wait for God my Savior; my God will hear me" (Micah 7:7).

HURT ROAD OR HOPE ROAD?

I've always loved Robert Frost's profound little poem called "The Road Not Taken." It's the closing words that frame so well the two kinds of choices we face when we lose one of our life anchors:

Two roads diverged in a wood, and I—
I took the one less traveled by,
And that has made all the difference.

The road that leads to more hurt is arguably the road more traveled. Because we follow our fear. Or our anger. Or our loneliness. Or our impatience. All powerful emotional pulls when the future is suddenly enveloped in fog. While the first steps on that road may bring some short-term relief or satisfaction, it will ultimately take us to compounding hurt and painful regrets.

But there is another road—the road that is usually "less traveled." On the front end, it's harder because you have to fight off the strong urges to panic, to "settle," to strike back, or to go for a quick but costly fix.

But there is real hope after your hurt when you make the choices that offer a healing way forward—without the "hangover" of regrets. We vote for hope when we follow four guidelines for decisions without regrets.

Stay in Touch with the Tower

United Airlines 232 was on a flight from Chicago to Denver when its number two engine failed, causing the loss of all of its hydraulic systems. In short, the plane would be considered impossible to fly. On that July day in 1989, it looked as if none of the 296 souls aboard would survive.

But somehow, Captain Al Haynes managed to maneuver the aircraft to the ground at the Sioux City, Iowa, airport. It cartwheeled across the tarmac and into a nearby cornfield. Amid fireballs and clouds of black smoke. Tragically, 112 passengers died that day. The miracle was that anyone survived—nearly two-thirds of the passengers.

Later, as Captain Haynes was hailed as a hero, he made sure his hero was recognized too. The flight controller who guided him every step of the way. Captain Haynes said perhaps the major reason he was able to bring his plane down at all was the "calm, steady voice in the tower."

In a sense, that's what has kept me from crashing in the wake of devastating losses. The calm, steady Voice from the tower. The God who has promised:

> Do not fear, for I have redeemed you; I have summoned you by name; you are mine. When you pass through the waters, I will be with you; when you pass through the rivers, they will not sweep over you. When you walk through the fire, you will not be burned…For I am the LORD, your God, the Holy One of Israel, your Savior (Isaiah 43:1-3).

My God has not promised I won't go through the flood and the fire. He has promised that I will come out safe on the other side—because He is with me every step of the way.

So as I face decisions about what to do in the face of great loss, it is vital that I stay in touch with my Flight Controller in the tower.

Because His calm and loving voice may be the only constant of my otherwise "up for grabs" world.

I hear His voice most clearly as I read what He's written. The Bible. Especially books like Psalms. And Proverbs. There I find guidance that saves me from the reckless choices toward which my feelings may pull me.

And if ever I need to pray a "pour out your heart" prayer to Him, it's in the fire and the flood of great loss. That's where to go with my fear. My anger. My loneliness. My impatience.

If I stay in constant touch with the tower, my Controller will steer me away from hurtful choices and toward the choices that offer hope. He will keep me from crashing.

Count the Cost

Jesus framed future-thinking decisions this way: First, sit down and estimate the cost. "What will going down this road cost me—sooner or later?" When we respond out of fear or anger, loneliness or impatience, we tend to forget the cost. We just want relief. But at what price?

Short-term fixes usually lead to long-term consequences. Short pleasure, long pain. So you ask questions like:

- What will the cost be to my relationship with God?

- How will this affect my reputation?

- What will the cost be to my close relationships?

- And to my relationship with God?

- How will this affect my financial future?

- What are all the possible downsides of doing this?

- Who will I hurt if I do this?

Years ago, we were staying near a beautiful Adirondack lake. The road around that lake offered ten miles of aroma-filled pine trees and scenic hills. Steep hills. Really steep when you're doing them on a ten-mile bike ride around the lake. Which we did.

Going down those hills was epic. You felt like you were flying. Definite "yee-hah!" moments.

One problem: As soon as you got to the bottom of that hill, there was another hill. Did I mention steep? I felt like my leg muscles were going to explode as I strained my way to the top.

If I had written a blog about that experience, I would have titled it "The Downhill Thrill…and the Uphill Bill!" Guess which one lasted longer? Definitely, the bill. The price you paid for those thrills.

The easy, human nature choices offer the initial "thrill" of some relief, some distraction from your loss. But the bill of regrets and additional hurt will last much longer than the thrill at the beginning.

That's why Jesus tells us to count the cost of our choices. Is this worth the bill?

Of course, every choice has consequences. Even right choices. But I'd far rather deal with the consequences of doing the right thing than the wrong thing.

But as we consider the life-building choices (rather than the life-scarring ones), here come the "yeah, buts." "Yeah, but if I do the right thing…" Then we start to think about all the "mights" and "coulds" that could follow. My observation is that most of our "mights" and "coulds" turn out to be "weren'ts." But still, there will be downstream effects from even the best of choices.

There's good news in the third guideline for a "no regrets" choice.

Trust God with the Consequences

The statement in the Bible is only ten words. But they provide, what is for me, a helpful answer to my "yeah, buts": "Offer right sacrifices, and put your trust in the LORD" (Psalm 4:5 ESV).

First, settle what's the "right" choice. That's where I try to line up my choices with my North Star—the Bible. Which choice is most consistent with what I know from God's Book? Because "Your word is a lamp for my feet, and a light on my path" (Psalm 119:105). Like my lantern in a dark campground, I can find light for my next step in the Bible.

Second, the right thing is often a "sacrifice." "Offer right sacrifices." More often than not, the cheap and easy choice is the wrong choice. When you do the right thing, the sacrifice is usually up front. The farther you go down that road, the more you reap its significant rewards.

When you do the wrong thing, it's usually easy at the beginning—and gets increasingly expensive as you go.

So you pay a price either way. But right choices have a short-term cost for long-term blessing. Wrong choices have a short-term benefit, but a cost that can last a lifetime.

The last part of the verse is the load-lightener for me. "And put your trust in the LORD." So what happens after you offer that right sacrifice? It's up to God from there! My Father who loves me will manage the consequences of my God-pleasing decisions.

Almighty God will fight my battles. Determining and doing the right thing is my job. The consequences of me doing the right thing are God's job.

So much for my "yeah, buts."

When I, or someone in our family, has an important decision to make, you'll often hear a four-word reminder. It is the fourth guideline for making choices that lead to hope rather than heartache.

Go with the Peace

That advice stems from this bottom line for decisions that will stand the test of time: "Let the peace of Christ rule in your hearts" (Colossians 3:15).

The word that's translated "rule" comes from the original Greek language the New Testament was written in. It means "be the umpire."

In baseball, the umpire is the one who calls players "safe" or "out." Sometimes, you'll see a manager nose-to-nose with an umpire, arguing over his call. But I've never seen an umpire lose the argument. The umpire is the final word.

So is the "peace of Christ."

I've come to understand that peace to be the direction I'm feeling most consistently when it's just Jesus and me discussing it. And there's usually a pull in a certain direction—and a diminishing pull in the other direction.

It's when other voices—including my own—start chiming in that I get confused again. But when I'm just laying my decision before Jesus, there's usually an inner peace about a certain way to go. And that sense is the "umpire" calling one choice "safe" and the other "out."

So after checking with my Flight Controller…and considering the cost…and trusting God with the consequences of doing the right thing—it's time to "go with the peace."

That's how I find myself in the blessing of God's plan rather than in the wilderness of my own.

ON THE OTHER SIDE OF THE TURBULENCE

It was our first time in Alaska. And the folks who had invited me to speak there were gracious enough to invite me to bring my whole family to the "Last Frontier." Unfortunately, it wasn't July when all those fancy cruises happen. No, it was February. Still very winter in Alaska.

At the end of my first week of speaking assignments, our children had to get back for school. A missionary pilot was prepared to fly them out of a small local airport to shuttle them to a flight that originated in Anchorage. I would stay longer to keep some other commitments.

I've never before—or since—helped push a plane out on the runway. But I did this night. The runway had frozen and refrozen—leaving a rutted ice washboard. We managed to get the plane in position for takeoff. I entrusted my precious cargo to God and a veteran bush pilot.

I waved goodbye and, honestly, was a little apprehensive as I watched Dick, our pilot, start that twin-engine aircraft down the icy runway. Karen was in the copilot seat and later told me that Dick was literally playing the engines back and forth to keep from sliding off the runway. Needless to say, it was one bumpy ride.

But scarier than the runway was the looming sight at the end of the runway—a tall stand of trees in the path of their speeding aircraft.

Karen held her breath. She was right up front where she could see everything.

And at the last second, Dick pulled back that stick and took his plane airborne. Just in time to skillfully clear the trees. It was finally time to breathe again.

Then, as they climbed above the clouds, they were bathed in a glorious rainbow of light. A breathtaking view of the Aurora Borealis—the stunning Northern Lights! A sight they would never forget.

Their harrowing flight had lifted them into a zone of incredible beauty.

That is what's happened to me since that devastating day when my baby left for heaven. It's been a bumpy, troubling flight at times. But I know my Pilot. I trust my Pilot. He's never crashed.

And I'm starting now to see emerging beauty, both in my soul and in my circumstances, that's on the other side of the harrowing ride.

It's a beauty we miss if we let our loss lead us into decisions that end up compounding our loss. But if we take that "road less traveled" and make hopeful decisions, they will lift us to a better place. Where the view makes the bumpy ride worth it.

CHAPTER 12

ONE SAFE PLACE

*Nothing...will ever be able to
separate us from the love of God.*

ROMANS 8:39 NLT

Your junior high years are usually turbulent enough. So who needs a tornado? Well, we got one.

My mom and dad and I had enough warning to hunker down in our basement. We knew when it was going through. That "roar like a freight train" you always hear people talk about in the news.

The clatter outside was our trash cans leaving us. And while there were a few pretty terrifying moments, our house was spared any significant damage. My junior high school was not.

We lived right across the football field from the school. And when we ventured out, we saw something new about it. It didn't have a roof anymore. A wave of disappointment swept over me (really?) as it dawned on me that we might have to skip school for a few days. That twister affected a lot of lives in our town.

Tornadoes always do. Several years ago, there was a real killer tornado in eastern Oklahoma. I watched a news report about a mother and her adult daughter, who lived right in the bull's-eye of the twister's path.

It was an F5, the rating reserved only for the most destructive storms. They could hear that deadly roar as they ran to the safe room they had in their house. They got the door secured just as that monster hit.

After a few minutes, they cautiously opened that heavy metal door. And gasped at what they saw. There was no house anymore. No neighborhood. Everywhere they looked, they saw how the storm had, in moments, changed everything.

This mother and daughter basically lost everything that afternoon. Except each other.

Because they knew their one safe place.

So did I. When the most devastating storm of my life went through, taking my greatest treasure on earth. The woman I have loved so much for so long. And there was no warning.

If it hadn't been for my "safe room," I don't know what I would have done.

HOPE IN THE PICTURE ON THE WALL

There is a picture that hangs on the wall in our living room. A picture that reminds me of my one safe place when it feels like everything else has suddenly been blown away. It hangs right over my baby's blue recliner. It's a picture I first saw many years ago as a six-year-old boy.

After my baby brother's sudden death, my nonchurchgoing dad decided he should take his other son to church somewhere. Sunday after Sunday, he would drop me off at the church closest to our apartment and just sit in the car, smoking and reading until I was finished.

They had what they called "junior church." And that's where I saw the picture. It was my first impression of the Jesus I hadn't heard about before.

The picture shows Jesus as a shepherd. He's leading a flock of sheep alongside a quiet mountain stream. And in His arms, a little lamb. Looking up at his shepherd as the shepherd looks lovingly at him.

And I said, "That's me! I'm the lamb in Jesus's arms!"

Not just then as a six-year-old boy. But on the darkest day of my life. Oh, how I needed my Shepherd. And He was there. Again, I was the lamb in His arms. My one safe place.

YOUR DARK VALLEY

Earlier in this book, we visited the biblical passage called "The Shepherd Psalm." And these words that have provided divine comfort for hurting people for centuries: "The LORD is my shepherd…though I walk through the valley of the shadow of death, I will fear no evil" (Psalm 23:1,4 NKJV).

Which raises the question, *"Why not?"* The surroundings are dark and dangerous. The reason is simple but decisive: "For You are with me."

Suddenly, on that heartbreaking May day, I was in the valley of the shadow of death. And, facing ultimate reality, one day I will be walking through the valley of the shadow of my own death.

And while the valley of that shadow is probably the darkest and most devastating, there are other dark valleys that shake us to our core too.

When the medical tests reveal a life-changing—or potentially life-ending—verdict. Or when the marriage that was once your dream collapses into the nightmare of separation or divorce. When a disaster destroys a lifetime of possessions and treasures.

For some, it's the valley of the shadow of financial disaster. Or the destruction of a fire or an accident or a natural disaster. The gut punch of being "downsized," laid off, or fired. Or the shadow cast by the rebellion of a son or daughter. The sadness of still being single when you were sure you'd be married by now. Or the pain of betrayal or breakup.

Each of us has—or will have—to walk through some of life's long, lonely valleys.

But we don't have to walk that perilous stretch alone: "I will fear no evil; for You are with me" (Psalm 23:4 NKJV). And Jesus "will stand and shepherd his flock in the strength of the LORD…and they will live securely" (Micah 5:4).

The vulnerable, frightened sheep is safe in the Shepherd's arms.

I know. Because everything I've ever believed about Jesus was validated by the biggest hurt and deepest valley of my life.

Even with the most incalculable loss of my life, Jesus is enough. That is hope. Indestructible hope.

Yes, I am still the lamb in His arms.

WHERE HOPE DROPS ANCHOR

As we started our hope journey in the early pages of this book, I offered a definition of what hope really is. After suggesting that "the hope has to be greater than life's most devastating losses."

So hope has to be more than wishful thinking. Or positive thoughts. Or sedating medication or stubborn determination. It must be a safe room so strong that it will still be standing when the F5 storm has blown away everything else.

So, hope is…a buoyant confidence that acknowledges the hurt, but anchors to an unseen, but certain, reality.

For me and for countless millions for 2,000 years, that has been the One the Bible calls the "Good Shepherd."

When Jesus rose from the dead three days after His crucifixion, He proved beyond any doubt that He is more powerful than the strongest of life's storms. And He went on to explain that His resurrection was more than just a historical or religious event. It was deeply personal. For anyone who entrusts their life into His hands: "Because I live, you also will live" (John 14:19).

Earlier, He described the total security of His "sheep": "I am the good shepherd. The good shepherd lays down his life for the sheep" (John 10:11).

And He did. When, on that cross, He loved us enough to pay the death penalty for our hijacking of our life from Him. And anyone who loves me enough to die for me is never going to turn His back on me.

Jesus went on to extend this bedrock guarantee: "My sheep…follow me. I give them eternal life, and they shall never perish; no one will snatch them out of my hand" (John 10:27-28).

That is the ultimate "unseen, but certain, reality" that extends beyond this life all the way into eternity. And it is "anchored" to the proven power of Jesus's resurrection from the dead.

It is no wonder, then, that He is later described as "our Lord Jesus, that great Shepherd of the sheep" (Hebrews 13:20).

That day in May when Karen went to be with Jesus was the best day of her life. And the worst day of mine. I could celebrate the glory she was experiencing in heaven. But I was still here. Without my amazing partner.

Because I've pinned all my eternal hopes on my death-crushing

Jesus, I know my forever "safe room" is secure. But what about my uncharted journey between here and heaven?

I've needed to know again the difference my Shepherd makes in the here and now, not just the "there and then." As I've revisited the Bible's promises about His day-to-day care, I've seen again that He is all I'll ever need for this season after the storm.

LOVING GUARANTEES FROM THE SHEPHERD

I'm grateful that the Bible reveals some compelling reasons for an unsinkable hope, anchored to the difference the shepherding of Jesus makes. This hope truly offers a "buoyant confidence." It is worth clinging to this "unseen, but certain, reality" to which my hope is anchored.

I've discovered seven loving guarantees that come from the Shepherd to His sheep. Added up, they decisively address our greatest fears—and any and all of life's hope robbers.

He Makes Sure You Have What You Need

The drought had been relentless, and the little dairy farm's well had gone dry.

My wife grew up on that little farm—no electricity, no running water. I kidded her about growing up like Laura Ingalls Wilder in the "little house on the prairie"—except a hundred years later.

Life was always hard on that farm. Even harder when their primary water source dried up. But that's when Jack and Betsy got to work.

When Karen first told me about them, I wondered if they were cousins. Not exactly. Jack and Betsy were her granddad's mules. The ones who pulled the wagon loaded with barrels, headed for the nearby spring.

Karen took me there years later. It was amazing. Water gushing horizontally out of a wall of rock. Her family would always come back with barrels full of water. Even in a drought. Even when the well was dry.

There are drought times in all of our lives—when our source for what we need dries up. The paycheck's suddenly not there—or not enough. The person who met so many of our needs either can't or won't. Something's happened to our home, our source of transportation, our health.

The "well" we depend on to meet our need has suddenly "gone dry." That's the seed for a crisis of hope.

Except for the Shepherd. The foundation of the Twenty-third Psalm—the Shepherd Psalm—is in the opening words: "The LORD is my shepherd, I shall not want" (verse 1 NKJV). That promise is echoed throughout the Bible. For example: "My God will meet all your needs according to the riches of his glory in Christ Jesus" (Philippians 4:19).

And then, Jesus's own words: "Do not worry, saying, 'What shall we eat?' or 'What shall we drink?' or 'What shall we wear?'...Your heavenly Father knows that you need them. But seek first his kingdom and his righteousness, and all these things will be given to you as well" (Matthew 6:31-33).

Sheep don't find their own pastures. Shepherds make sure they know where there's grazing, and they make sure their flock "shall not want." So it is with the Good Shepherd.

When our well dries up, His spring is still flowing. Our adult daughter loves to tell about the Thanksgiving when the Hutchcrafts had nothing to buy groceries with. So the day before Thanksgiving, we met with our kids and explained that we wouldn't be having Thanksgiving dinner this year. But we did pray together that, if it was God's will, that He would somehow provide for us.

That same afternoon, the doorbell rang. It was a Bible study group from our church, none of whom had any idea about our need. They had come with boxes and bags of groceries, including everything a family would need for a full Thanksgiving dinner!

To this day, our daughter points to that amazing moment as the epicenter of a great faith in God's provision that has sustained her ever since.

When the money we would usually buy groceries with "dried up," God still kept His promise. He went to the spring.

He is infinitely creative in His means of providing. The Bible shows us He's a God who provides water from a rock, manna from heaven, two meals a day delivered by ravens to his prophet in the wilderness. He kept His people's shoes from wearing out with 40 years of walking in the wilderness and provided food for 5,000 from one lunch.

After three years of itinerant ministry with His disciples, Jesus asked them, "When I sent you without purse, bag or sandals, did you lack anything?" (Luke 22:35). We should not be surprised at their brief but revealing reply: "'Nothing,' they answered." After many years of doing life with my Shepherd, if He asked me a similar question, my honest answer would be the same as that of those disciples.

I read once about the orphans of war that American GIs found as they liberated French villages during World War II. These shellshocked children were taken to army hospitals for some love and care. Unfortunately, many of them could not get to sleep at night, no matter what the nurses tried.

Then the army psychiatrists had an idea. They suspected that these children, who had gone to sleep hungry so many nights, couldn't sleep because of their fear of having nothing to eat the next day. Their solution? Give each child a slice of bread to hold as they went to sleep. It worked! Because what they would need tomorrow was already in their hand.

With an all-powerful Shepherd who has promised "we shall not want," what we will need for tomorrow is as good as in our hand.

He Will Carry You When You Have No Strength to Go On

There we were, standing at the bottom of those steep steps at the United States Capitol Building. Our youngest son was only three. I can't imagine how daunting the challenge must have looked—climbing all those stairs with three-year-old legs.

But the little guy made it all the way to the top!

Because his father carried him where he could never have gone himself.

And that's the Shepherd's second hope-giving guarantee: He will carry you when you have no strength to go on.

That was me when, in one life-rocking moment, I was suddenly facing life without her. After doing my whole adult life with her. It was a hill too steep for me to climb.

But that's when I experienced the realness of God's words: "The LORD your God carried you, as a father carries his son" (Deuteronomy 1:31). It's not the first time. Throughout my life, in the times when I have hit a wall and just couldn't walk any further, my Shepherd's strength has carried me.

I've learned that God can do the most when I have nothing left to give.

In our seasons of shattering loss, our hope of picking up the pieces and going on can be shattered too. Unless we know we can always reach up with both arms and say, "Daddy, carry me." And He will. He has.

He says, in a couple of my anchor verses: "I have upheld [you] since your birth, and have carried [you] since you were born. Even to your old age and gray hairs I am he, I am he who will sustain you. I have made you and I will carry you; I will sustain you and I will rescue you" (Isaiah 46:3-4).

That is the ultimate "whole life insurance policy"!

He Will Restore You When Your Soul Is Drained and Battered

You need them after a fire. You need them after a flood. Someone who knows how to restore what the disaster has damaged.

We all need someone who can restore a wounded, damaged heart. Because when one of life's knockout punches hits us, it takes a toll on our soul. We feel depleted. Defeated. Disillusioned. Disoriented. Discouraged. Like Rocky, staggering to his corner, beat up and barely able to go on.

Rocky has Mick, his manager, who, before the next round, has him ready to fight again.

I have Jesus in my corner. In the times when I learn I have been betrayed by people I really trusted. When I'm spent by weeks of giving everything I have to an almost round-the-clock mission to hurting people.

Most of all, when my heart was shattered because I would never again see or hold my Karen this side of heaven.

I felt like my soul was bullet-riddled. It was then I heard again the promise of my Shepherd: "He leads me beside the still waters. He restores my soul" (Psalm 23:2-3 NKJV).

Another guarantee from the Shepherd…He will restore you when your soul is drained and battered.

Hope means things will not always be this way. There will be a spring, no matter how dark and cold the winter. And "restore" means my soul will be brought back to life.

As I cried out to my Shepherd for soul repair, He reminded me of the words that precede "He restores my soul." It says, "He leads me beside the still waters."

A car has to go into the shop to be repaired. My computer has to leave where I am working for it to be fixed. I realized I needed to stop if I was going to be restored. Because His healing hand does its work when we are standing still.

One week after Karen's homegoing, I wrote in my grief journal: "I must get away by myself to try to feel my feelings, hear God's voice, and get Jesus's perspective on this land without a map."

So, for the next two weeks, I hit pause on my relentless schedule and just hunkered down to hear from Jesus. And to pour out my heart to the only One who could really understand. The only One I didn't have to be strong for.

As my heart was crying out, "Where do I go from here?" I planted my feet on His promise from the Twenty-third Psalm again: "He leads me beside the still waters. He restores my soul; He leads me in the paths of righteousness for His name's sake" (verse 3 NKJV).

So I asked Him where to read in His Word, the Bible. I immersed myself in those Scripture passages, seeking direction. I loaded up on music that reminded me of His love and majesty. I dumped my raw thoughts and feelings into the grief journal I had started.

I was living the promise that "God is our refuge and strength, an ever-present help in trouble." And living His invitation: "Be still, and know that I am God" (Psalm 46:1,10).

I've learned that, if we will set aside "be still" time at the beginning of each new day, the Shepherd will actually do daily repairs: "That is why we never give up. Though our bodies are dying, our spirits are being renewed every day" (2 Corinthians 4:16 NLT).

One of America's most prolific hymn writers—of some 9,000 hymns—was a blind believer named Fanny Crosby. While she could not see physically, her spiritual sight was sharper than most of us who can see. It is no surprise she would write some beautiful words to describe the soul-healing touch of Jesus:

> Down in the human heart, crushed by the tempter,
> Feelings lie buried that grace can restore:

Touched by a loving heart, wakened by kindness,
Chords that are broken will vibrate once more.

He Will Bring You Back When You Start to Wander

Our adult daughter will never let me forget what happened when she was four years old. Because she can't seem to forget it.

My wife and I took her grocery shopping with us. We must have been looking briefly at some potential purchase because Miss Independent Firstborn decided to go on ahead of us. She saw interesting items. She kept going. All of a sudden, she looked around and realized she had wandered too far. She was lost. And crying.

It must have seemed like a long time to her. Actually, we found her right away. She couldn't find her parents.

Our four-year-old little girl never intended to get lost. She didn't run away. She just wandered away. Just like sheep drifting away from their shepherd—and suddenly lost. And just like us getting away from God.

Often that drift starts when we are hit by one of life's hope-draining losses. Many have ended up farther from God than they ever dreamed because their hurt got them wandering.

That's why I love the promise of another of the Shepherd's guarantees: He will bring you back when you start to wander.

He says: "You are my sheep…I will search for the lost and bring back the strays. I will bind up the injured and strengthen the weak" (Ezekiel 34:31,16).

Jesus is the Shepherd who will "go after the lost sheep until he finds it" (Luke 15:4). He skillfully, lovingly, relentlessly pursues us when, for whatever reason, we are drifting from His love.

That's very good news for all of us sheep. And really good news for those whose heart is heavy for a son or daughter or loved one who's away from the Shepherd.

He brings His lost sheep home.

And…

He Will Always Keep You Safe

In God's words, "He will stand and shepherd his flock in the strength of the LORD…and they will live securely" (Micah 5:4). Jesus stands between me and the predators, the traps, and the dangers.

We are never more vulnerable than when we are hit by a painful loss. I am so thankful for God's guarantee that I am guarded by an all-knowing, all-loving, all-powerful Shepherd. And that's a whole lot of hope.

Years ago, my wife had the opportunity to take our daughter and son-in-law on a tour of her childhood. Down the country roads to the places where her memories lived.

One of those is near the spring I referenced earlier. She took them through the woods to a cave by a stream. The entrance was just above their heads—so they didn't go in. After about 20 minutes of stories, they moved on.

That night, back at their motel, our son-in-law ran some of the video he had filmed that afternoon. At one point, my daughter said, "Stop! Go back, please." As the video paused, they studied the cave for a moment. "Guys, look closely just inside the cave entrance." That's when they saw a dark form and the eyes glowing dimly in the dark.

There had been a mountain lion just above their heads the whole time they were there!

When they called to tell me about it, I said, "I wonder how many times there have been 'cats that never pounced'? Maybe in heaven God will roll the video and show us all kinds of dangers He's protected us from—that we never even knew were there."

All day. All night. All our lives. We are safe because of our Shepherd.

He Will Lead and Go Ahead of You into Your Unknown

It would probably be an exaggeration to call my sense of direction a "sense" at all. The stories of my getting lost are the stuff of family legends.

So on our family trips, Karen and I each knew our assignment: Me pilot, she navigator. Her sense of direction was as highly developed as my ability to get lost.

On the day she went to heaven, I felt totally lost. We had traveled life together our whole adult lives. The prospect of doing life alone was a long, dark road. Without a map.

But I had a promise—a guarantee—from the Shepherd I had come to love as a child. The Shepherd Psalm assures us that "He leads me in the paths of righteousness [or "right paths," as another translation says] for His name's sake" (Psalm 23:3 NKJV). Jesus Himself assures us of His guidance when He affirms that "my sheep listen to my voice; I know them, and they follow me" (John 10:27).

In this time when I've needed guidance more, I've concluded that the more clueless I am, the closer Jesus is. Or maybe it's more about me staying closer to Him than I ever have. Because I've never needed Him so much.

Some words from my grief journal in those first weeks alone document what it's been like with Him on this journey:

> Three weeks ago tonight. My last "I love you" to my baby—and her to me. Jesus, it hit me this morning what I've lived of You these past three weeks. It is You literally taking my hand, as I would a lost little boy, and leading me moment by moment through my day. Leading me to amazing verse after amazing verse. Leading me to journal. Leading me to turn on the radio for a timely song. To listen to CDs. To read some incredible note in a card. To pray about something. To visit Karen's grave with flowers.

It's endless. Oh yes, my Shepherd is all over me, keeping
His promise to walk with me "through the valley of the
shadow of death."

Now it's been two years—hard to believe. But He continues to lead
my hours, then days, now months, slowly revealing the shape of my
future in this unexplored territory.

I am living the truth of a powerful promise for the times when a
great loss has made the future the great unknown: "I will lead the blind
by ways they have not known, along unfamiliar paths I will guide them;
I will turn the darkness into light before them and make the rough
places smooth…I will not forsake them" (Isaiah 42:16).

The uncertainty of our future after a life-changing loss is a major
reason we lose hope. The certainty of a future orchestrated and revealed
by the One who loves us most is a major reason to keep hope alive.

What's exciting is not just that He will guide us into the unknown…
He will actually go ahead of us into the unknown! That's what shepherds do!

Speaking of the Good Shepherd, the Bible says that "when he has
brought out all his own, he goes ahead of them" (John 10:4). So Jesus
is already in my tomorrows, preparing the way. Anticipating needs.
Dealing with dangers.

Everywhere I walk, I will find the Shepherd's footprint. He will
always get there ahead of me.

No wonder the Bible says, literally hundreds of times, "Do not be
afraid." I don't know what my future holds. But I know Who holds
my future.

He Will Stay Close to Our Children and Grandchildren

Often our hope struggle is not about us. It's about our children.
Our grandchildren. It is their choices, the dangers on their road.

It is no secret that the older they get, the less influence and control we have over the choices they're making. We know where some of those roads go, and we don't want anyone we love to go there.

As our world becomes more morally and physically perilous for the generations following us, it is so hope affirming to hear another guarantee of the Shepherd's care: "He tends his flock like a shepherd; he gathers the lambs in his arms and carries them close to his heart" (Isaiah 40:11).

So we have the Shepherd's guarantee that He will stay close to our children and grandchildren.

I love the picture of Jesus carrying our three children and nine grandchildren "close to His heart." Because He can go with them where I cannot go.

So I have found myself actually putting their names in that promise when I pray. Replacing "the lambs" with the names of our precious next generations.

He watches over them better than I ever could. He knows when one may be starting down a dark road. He knows what they need. And His shepherding promises reach beyond just my own life to cover their lives too—carrying them, restoring them, leading them, keeping them safe, bringing them back.

THE GAME CHANGER

I was in my office when someone ran in and said, "You need to turn on your TV. There's been a plane crash on the Hudson River!"

My first thought: lives lost. When I turned on the news, I couldn't believe what I was seeing. The plane, largely intact, floating on the river, all 155 passengers on the wings, awaiting rescue. They all survived. It would come to be called "the miracle on the Hudson."

US Airways Flight 1549 was just taking off from LaGuardia Airport when it struck a flock of Canadian geese. Suddenly, the plane had lost all engine power.

Captain Chesley (Sully) Sullenberger was faced now with the most critical decision of his long career in aviation. Try to get back to the airport? Or try to ditch in the Hudson River?

The rest is aviation history. Probably the most amazing and successful "ditch" of an airplane ever.

What the passengers did not know until later was who this pilot was who held their lives in his hands. Sully Sullenberger was a veteran fighter pilot, then commercial pilot for 20 years. He had also been a glider pilot and was an expert on airline safety.

They didn't get to choose their pilot that day. But if they had known what lay ahead, they would have picked Sully Sullenberger. Possibly the only pilot who could have landed them all safely.

For all my years of flying, I've never been able to choose the pilot of my plane. But I did get to choose the pilot of my life.

Like all of us humans, I first tried to fly it myself. That was a bad idea. I was never meant to decide where my life went—and you could tell by the mess, and the mistakes I made.

No, my life was supposed to be piloted by the One who gave me my life in the first place. Speaking of Jesus, the Bible says we were "created through him and for him" (Colossians 1:16).

Mark Twain said there are two important days in a person's life: the day he was born and the day he finds out why. We all know the first one. Most of us spend our whole life trying to figure out the second one—the why.

But the answer is right there in the Bible in six words: *created through him and for him*. Problem: I added three words of my own. *Living for me*. It's that sin thing the Bible talks about. Which isn't breaking some religion's rules. It's me hijacking my life from the Pilot in charge.

We've all done it. God says, "All have sinned" (Romans 3:23). And with us at the controls, we'll keep ending up at wrong destinations. And ultimately crashing. The ultimate destination of a life I run is a forever away from God.

But one day I answered the wake-up call from God. I realized that the very God I had disregarded and pushed to the edge still loved me. So much that He didn't want to lose me.

But the only way I could ever belong to the One I was made for was to have the penalty paid for the hijacking of my life. And the penalty for hijacking is death. And in this case, the spiritual death of forever separation from a God who's perfect.

Now comes the part where I let go of the controls and make Jesus the Pilot of my life. He captured my heart with the greatest act of love in human history.

He did the dying for the sinning I had done against Him. Still blows me away. When He let them nail Him to that cross, He actually "suffered for our sins…He died for sinners to bring you safely home to God" (1 Peter 3:18 NLT).

Nobody ever loved me like that. I decided to put my life in the hands of the One who loves me most. And the One who is so powerful that He beat what has beaten every other person who ever lived: death.

The clincher for me was that Jesus blew the doors off death and walked out of His grave under His own power. So when He says, "Whoever believes in the Son [Me] has eternal life" (John 3:36), I know He can deliver on that promise. He can give us eternal life because He proved He has eternal life.

He's standing there with open arms, waiting for each of us to take what He died to give us. But it's hard getting our attention.

Until one of life's hammers hits. Until we lose someone or something that reminds us that we aren't in control after all. Until there's something too big for us to fix...to change...or to handle.

That's when we lost sheep start to realize we're lost. When we realize the Great Shepherd has come looking for us. And when we experience that little two-letter word that changes everything, including our eternity: *my*.

The Lord is *my* Shepherd. Not just *the* Shepherd, but *my* Shepherd. When it finally dawns that, in the Bible's words, "[He] loved me and gave himself for me" (Galatians 2:20).

This Jesus has walked with me through the darkest, deepest, loneliest valley of my life. All I can say is, "He's enough." He has been hope for me when nothing else in all the world could have been more powerful than what I had lost.

When we have Jesus, we really do have "an anchor for the soul, firm and secure" (Hebrews 6:19).

Even when it's time to walk "the valley of the shadow of death." Like it says, "I will fear no evil" because "you are with me" (Psalm 23:4).

That is hope that is stronger than every hurt. Every tragedy. Every loss. Even death itself.

Because it's not just hope for now.

It's hope forever.

If you want to know more about a personal relationship with Jesus, life's one "unlosable" love, visit…

ChatAboutJesus.com

You can chat online, send a text message, or call to talk with someone.

ABOUT THE AUTHOR

Ron Hutchcraft is a veteran ministry leader and speaker, and founder and president of Ron Hutchcraft Ministries and On Eagle's Wings Native American youth outreach. He is the author of *A Life That Matters*, *Peaceful Living in a Stressful World*, *The Battle for a Generation*, and more. His popular radio feature, *A Word with You*, is heard daily on over 1,300 outlets and in the world's five most-spoken languages. Ron and his late wife Karen have three children and nine grandchildren.

Facebook @ronhutchcraftministries
Twitter @ronhutchcraft
YouTube HutchcraftMinistries
Instagram @ronhutchcraft
Email: ron@hutchcraft.com

Subscribe to Ron's daily email devotional or blog:

hutchcraft.com/subscribe

More resources from Ron Hutchcraft:

hutchcraft.com

HopeWhenYourHeartIsBreaking.com

To learn more about Harvest House books and
to read sample chapters, visit our website:

www.harvesthousepublishers.com

HARVEST HOUSE PUBLISHERS
EUGENE, OREGON